Mission Statements for College Libraries

CLIP Note #5

Compiled by

Larry Hardesty
Director of Library Services
Eckerd College

Jamie Hastreiter
Systems Planning/Serials Coordinator
Eckerd College

David Henderson
Instructional Services/Collection Management Coordinator
Eckerd College

College Library Information Packet Commitee
College Libraries Section
Association of College and Research Libraries
a division of the American Library Association

Published by the Association of College and Research Libraries
a division of the American Library Association
50 East Huron Street
Chicago, IL 60611

ISBN 0-8389-6944-5

The paper used in this publication meets the minimum requirements of American National Standards for Information Sciences--Permanence of Paper for Printed Library Materials, ANSI Z39.48-1984. ∞

Printed in the United States of America.

TABLE OF CONTENTS

INTRODUCTION

Importance of the Study

Efforts to define and articulate the purposes of the college library have become increasingly important in recent years as budgets have become more strained—the result of economic adversity in higher education and the introduction of new services. During the past decade, college libraries have had to compete more actively to secure their share of the institutional budget while attempting to offer new services. As these new services, for example, online searching and computer software distribution, have become available, college librarians have been forced to consider how these services can best support the purposes of the college library. Adding to their difficulties, college librarians have had to contend with the "University-Library Syndrome," a condition, described by Evan Farber, in which the purposes of the college library are confused with those of the university library.[1]

The 1975 "Standards for College Libraries" recommend that at each institution a "clear and explicit statement of derivative library objectives is prepared and promulgated so that all members of the college community can understand and evaluate the appropriateness and effectiveness of library activities."[2] In addition, several regional accreditation agencies require as part of the accreditation process a written statement of the philosophy, goals, and objectives of the library as they relate to the overall philosophy of the parent institution. Nevertheless, a preliminary survey revealed that many, if not most, college libraries have not developed such a statement.

Objective of the Study

As described elsewhere, the College Library Information Packet Notes program is intended to "provide college and small university libraries with state-of-the-art reviews and current documentation on library practices and procedures of relevance to them."[3] The purpose of this particular CLIP Notes, therefore, is to gather basic data and sample documentation related to the general purposes of college libraries. These general purposes may be described variously as "mission statements," "statements of purpose," "goal statements," or "statements of objectives." The term used in this publication for these documents is "mission statements." The documents published are intended to provide examples of various philosophical statements outlining the purposes of particular college libraries. They are intended to provide impetus and guidance for other college libraries to develop or refine their own mission statements.

The Survey Sample and Methodology

During the fall of 1984, the authors wrote twelve library directors for informal responses regarding college library mission statements. Based on their responses, we concluded that a more in-depth study would be useful. Grady Morein, chair of the A C R L College Libraries Section CLIP Notes committee, provided the authors with a list of 181 institutions whose library directors had previously agreed to respond to CLIP Notes surveys. The colleges surveyed included those institutions defined by the Carnegie Council on Policy Studies in Higher Education in 1976 as either: 1) Comprehensive Universities and Colleges I, or 2) Liberal Arts Colleges I.[4] By mid-April, 132 responses had been received for a response rate of 72.9 percent. The survey results were tabulated and analyzed through use of the Prime computer at Eckerd College and version 9.0 of the Statistical Package for the Social Sciences.

Survey Results

The survey revealed that slightly over half the respondents (seventy-four) had developed a mission statement (see question #13). This percentage is misleading since some of the mission statements consisted of one or two sentences or, at most, a paragraph. Some respondents also included in this category collection development and other statements.

For those libraries with mission statements, whether or not a committee was used, the library director most frequently served as the primary drafter and the other librarians acted most frequently as reviewers. If a committee was used, most frequently it was the regular faculty library committee, chaired and given its charge by the library director. If a committee was not used, as was the case at approximately half the responding libraries, the library director most frequently wrote the mission statement. Some totals may be larger than the number of responding libraries because a few library directors answered, obviously in error, both questions #15 and #16.

Librarians formally adopted or approved approximately two-thirds (forty-nine) of the mission statements. The chief academic officer formally adopted or approved forty-three percent (thirty-two). The faculty senate or equivalent formally adopted or approved only thirteen percent (ten). Some sixteen percent (twelve) were never formally adopted or approved by any group or individual.

As indicated by the responses to question #18, the library director provided the primary initiative for the development of the mission statement. Other reasons, such as an institutional or a library self-study, ranked high in prompting the development of a mission statement. Seldom did classroom faculty prompt the development of a mission statement. Most frequently the statement took from one month to less than four months to develop, and it is reviewed annually.

2

The respondents generally ranked highly the use of the mission statement for: 1) relating the purposes of the library to the objectives of the teaching faculty, administrators, and students; 2) improving library services; and 3) conducting collection development. They generally ranked low use of the mission statement to support staff expansion or reallocation and improvement of the physical plant.

A majority of the respondents (almost entirely library directors) who had mission statements viewed the effort expended in developing the statements as worthwhile or very worthwhile. They generally believed that their fellow librarians, administrators, and teaching faculty viewed the development of a library mission statement as important. The library directors, however, tended to see the development of a library mission statement as less important to the teaching faculty than to themselves or to other librarians and college administrators.

Those library directors without mission statements provided a number of comments as to why they had not developed them. Many believed that such statements are too general or too political to be useful, and are usually ignored by everyone. Understandably, they considered the development of a mission statement as unimportant, and they believed that other groups at their institution shared their attitude.

A number of questions go unanswered by this brief overview of the descriptive statistics. For example, further analysis revealed statistically significant differences in student enrollments and materials acquisitions between those libraries with and without mission statements. In addition, the authors used multivariate analysis to examine possible relationships between the factors involved in the development of the mission statements and the attitudes of the library directors. The authors plan future publications in the professional literature to elaborate on the results of these analyses. For additional information, the reader should contact one of the authors of this publication.

This publication consists of five sections. The bulk of the publication, of course, is the sample documents provided by the respondents. In addition, the compilers have included the descriptive statistics that resulted from the survey, statements from the various regional accreditation agencies regarding college library mission statements, a reprint of "The Mission of an Undergraduate Library (Model Statement)," and, finally, the letters used as part of the survey. The compilers hope that this CLIP Notes publication will stimulate further thought about the purposes of the college library, which, in turn, we hope will result in development of additional college library missions statements.

REFERENCES

1. Evan Ira Farber, "College Librarians and the University-Library Syndrome," in The Academic Library: Essays in Honor of Guy R. Lyle, eds. Evan Ira Farber and Ruth Walling (Metuchen, New Jersey: Scarecrow Press, 1974), pp. 12-23.

2. "Standards for College Libraries," College & Research Libraries News 36 (October 1975): 278.

3. P. Grady Morein, "What is a CLIP Note?" College & Research Libraries News 46 (May 1985): 226.

4. Carnegie Council on Policy Studies in Higher Education. A Classification of Higher Education, rev. ed., Berkeley, California: The Carnegie Foundation for the Advancement of Teaching, 1976.

ACKNOWLEDGEMENTS

The success of a CLIP Notes publication is due to those librarians who took the time to respond to the survey. The compilers hope that these librarians will find this CLIP Notes a useful resource. In this way, the efforts of both the compilers and respondents will be rewarded.

8-27-85

CLIP Notes Survey (Results)

CLIP NOTES SURVEY

COLLEGE LIBRARY MISSION STATEMENTS

Directions
    If your library has developed a mission or similar statement, you will be asked how and why the statement was developed and how it is used. If your library has not developed such statement, you will be asked to provide informaiton as to why such a statement has not been developed.

Your cooperation is greatly appreciated.

A.   General Information: Please complete the following information before proceeding to the questions relating to the mission statements.

1)   Name:_____ 2) Date:_____ _____

3)   Position:_____

4)   Institution:_____

5)   Address:_____

6)   Approximate full-time equivalent (FTE) student enrollment of your institution (Fall 1984): Average: 2,429; Smallest: 219; Largest: 7,643

7)   Number of full-time equivalent (FTE) librarians at your institution (Fall 1984): Average: 7.8; Smallest: 1; Largest: 38

8)   Approximate number of book volumes, excluding bound periodicals, in you library (Fall 1984): Average: 230,653; Smallest: 79,000; Largest: 940,000

9)   Approximate number of current periodical subscriptions (Fall 1984): Average: 1,329; Smallest: 520; Largest: 3,667

10) Approximate annual library acquisition rate for books during 1983-84: Average: 6,651; Smallest: 407; Largest: 40,000

11) Approximate total library operating expenditures for your library for 1983-84 fiscal year: Average: $684,348; Smallest: $125,000; Largest: $3,385,817

12) Approximate total library operating expenditures for your library for 1983-84 fiscal year as a percent of general and educational institutional expenditures: Library expenditures divided by general and educational expenditures = Average: 4.29; Smallest: 1; Largest: 9.9

B. Mission Statement Information: General

13) Has your library developed a mission statement, statement of
objectives or similar statement?

    a)   <u>74</u> Yes: Please answer questions #14 through #25 and
return this survey form with an <u>example</u> of the
statment.

    b)   <u>58</u> No: Please skip to question #26 and continue.

C. Mission Statement Information: Development and Use

14) Who was involved in the <u>development</u> of the statement?
(check all that apply)

primary drafter(s)	reviewer(s)	
<u>66</u>	<u>14</u>	Library Director
<u>16</u>	<u>18</u>	Assistant Director(s) and/or Senior Librarian(s)
<u>24</u>	<u>41</u>	Librarians
<u>4</u>	<u>15</u>	Classroom Faculty Member(s)
<u>3</u>	<u>28</u>	Administrator(s) (specify title(s))
<u>2</u>	<u>9</u>	Student(s)
<u>4</u>	<u>17</u>	Other(s) (specify)

15) If a committee was used, was it . . . (check all that apply—if no
committee was used, skip to question 16.)

    a)   <u>24</u> A Regular Faculty Library Committee
           <u>10</u> A Special Committee Formed for this Purpose
           <u>12</u> Other (specify)

    b)   <u>21</u> Chaired by the Library Director
           <u>7</u> Chaired by a Librarian
           <u>15</u> Chaired by a Classroom Faculty Member
           <u>2</u> Chaired by an Administrator
           <u>1</u> Other (specify)

    c)   <u>22</u> Given a charge by the Library Director
           <u>7</u> Given a charge by an Administrator
           <u>2</u> Given a charge by another Committee
           <u>8</u> No Charge Given
           <u>3</u> Other (specify)

16) If no committee was used, who wrote the statement? (check all that apply)

   <u>31</u> Library Director
   <u>8</u> Another Librarian (specify title)
   <u>0</u> Administrator (specify title)
   <u>0</u> Classroom Faculty Member
   <u>5</u> Other (specify)

17) Was the statement formally adopted or approved by the . . . (check all that apply)

   <u>49</u> Librarians
   <u>10</u> Faculty Senate or equivalent
   <u>32</u> Chief Academic Officer (Dean, Provost, Vice-President of Academic Affairs, or equivalent)
   <u>12</u> President
   <u>4</u> Board of Trustees or equivalent
   <u>0</u> Student Government
   <u>13</u> Other (specify)
   <u>12</u> Never formally adopted or approved

18) What prompted the development of the statement? <u>Rank</u> in order of importance, i.e. 1, 2, 3, etc., with 1 being the most important reason.

   a. Part of regional accreditation process (rank, frequency): 1) 12; 2) 9; 3) 7; 4) 1. Average:= 1.9
   b. Desire to comply with "Standards for College Libraries" (rank, frequency): 1) 5; 2) 8; 3) 8; 4) 2. Average:= 2.3
   c. Initiative of the Library Director (rank, frequency): 1) 36; 2) 9; 3) 3. Average:= 1.3
   d. Initiative of Member(s) of Classroom Faculty (rank, frequency): 1) 1; 5) 5. Average:= 4.3
   e. Initiative of Administrator (President, etc., specify): 1) 10; 2) 2; 4) 5. Average:= 2.0
   f. Initiative of Students (rank,frequency): 6) 3. Average:= 6.0
   g. Other (specify) (rank, frequency): 1) 10; 2) 4; 4) 1; 7) 1. Average:= 1.8
   h. Do Not Know (rank, frequency): 1) 6. Average:= 1.0

19) Approximately how long did it take to develop the statement from initial draft to adoption? (check one)

   <u>9</u> Less than a week
   <u>15</u> A week to less than a month
   <u>23</u> A month to less than four months
   <u>7</u> Four months to less than an academic year
   <u>8</u> An academic year
   <u>4</u> More than an academic year (specify)
   <u>6</u> Do Not Know

20) How often is the statement reviewed? (check one)

<u>1</u> Each semester
<u>27</u> Annually
<u>16</u> In conjunction with accreditation process (specify frequency)
<u>26</u> Other (specify)

21) How is the statement used? <u>Rank</u> in order of importance, i.e. 1,2,3, etc.

    a. To guide improvement of services (rank, frequency): 1) 17; 2) 12; 3) 4; 4) 6; 5) 4; 6) 3. Average= 2.5
    b. To guide collection development (rank, frequency): 1) 19; 2) 10; 3) 3; 4) 3; 5) 6; 6) 4; 8) 1. Average= 2.7
    c. To guide expansion of staff (rank, frequency): 1) 2; 3) 3; 6) 5; 7) 7; 8) 1. Average:= 5.4
    d. To guide reallocation of staff (rank,frequency): 1) 2; 3) 3; 4) 2; 5) 1; 6) 3; 7) 3; 8) 4; 9) 1. Average:= 5.5
    e. To guide improvement of physical plant (rank, frequency): 1) 5; 2) 1; 4) 1; 5) 4; 6) 2; 7) 3; 8) 3; 9) 3. Average:= 5.2
    f. To relate the purposes of the library to objectives of the teaching faculty (rank, frequency): 1) 21; 2) 11; 3) 12; 4) 4; 5) 1; 6) 1; 7) 1. Average:= 2.2
    g. To relate the purposes of the library objectives of the college administrators (rank, frequency): 1) 13; 2) 7; 3) 6; 4) 6; 5) 2 7) 1; 8) 2; 9) 1. Average:= 2.9
    h. To relate the purposes of the library to the student needs (rank, frequency): 1) 14; 2) 11; 3) 8; 4) 7; 5) 2; 6) 2; 8) 2. Average:=2.7
    i. To relate the purposes of the library to the accreditation requirements of outside evaluators (specify evaluators) (rank, frequency): 1) 10; 2) 3; 3) 8; 4) 4; 5) 3; 8) 2; 9) 6. Average:=3.9
    j. Other (specify) (rank, frequency): 1) 13; 2) 1; 5) 1. Average:= 1.3

22) In your opinion, was the effort expended in developing the statement worthwhile? (Please circle the response that <u>best</u> reflects your opinion.)

	Very Worthwhile			Not Worthwhile		No Opinion
Rank	5	4	3	2	1	0
Frequency	23	24	14	2	1	10

Average: 4.0

23) In your opinion, how important is the statement to the librarians at your institution? (Please circle the response that best reflects your opinion.)

	Very Important			Not Important		No Opinion
Rank	5	4	3	2	1	0
Frequency	10	24	22	10	4	4

Average: 3.4

24) In your opinion, how important is the statement to the administrators at your institution? (Please circle the response that best reflects your opinion.)

	Very Important			Not Important		No Opinion
Rank	5	4	3	2	1	0
Frequency	8	15	27	10	9	5

Average: 3.0

25) In your opinion, how important is the statement to the teaching faculty at your institution? (Please circle the response that best reflects your opinion.)

	Very Important			Not Important		No Opinion
Rank	5	4	3	2	1	0
Frequency	2	16	23	13	15	5

Average: 2.7

NOTE: If you answered YES to question #13, please answer no further questions and skip to the comments section on the last page. Return the completed survey form with simple mission statement documents in the stamped self-addressed envelope. Thank you.

D. Mission Statement Information: Libraries Without Mission Statements

26) Check the reason(s) a library mission statement or similar statement
has been developed at your institution. (Rank in order of importance,
i.e. 1, 2, 3, etc., with being the most important reason.)

    a. Too time consuming (rank, frequency): 1) 7; 2) 2; 3) 4; 4) 2;
       5) 1; 6) 1. Average: 2.5
    b. Too political (explain) (rank, frequency): 1) 1; 7) 2. Average: 5.0
    c. Mission statements are too general to be useful (rank, frequency):
       1) 10; 2) 8; 3) 2; 4) 1. Average: 1.7
    d. Mission statements are usually ignored by everyone (rank,
       frequency): 1) 4; 2) 7; 3) 3; 4) 1; 5) 1. Average: 2.3
    e. Mission statements unnecessarily limit the role and activities of
       the library (rank, frequency): 1) 1; 2) 3; 3) 1; 5) 2; 7) 1.
       Average 3.4
    f. Mission statements are seldom useful in obtaining additional library
       funds (rank, frequency): 1) 6; 2) 5; 3) 2; 4) 1; 5) 1.
       Average: 2.1
    g. Mission statements seldom take into account the level of
       resources available to the library (rank, frequency): 1) 1; 2) 6;
       3) 3; 4) 1. Average: 2.4
    h. Development of mission statements create divisive arguments (rank,
       frequency): 3) 1; 6) 2; 8) 1. Average: 5.8
    i. Other (comment) (rank, frequency): 1) 27; 2) 2; 3) 3; 4) 1.
       Average: 1.3

27) Has an accreditation association ever asked for or recommended the
development of a mission statement or similar statement for your
library? __4__ Yes; __38__ No   __14__ Do Not Know

28) How important is the development of a library mission statement to
you? (Please circle the response that best reflects your opinion.)

	Very Important		Not Important			No Opinion
Rank	5	4	3	2	1	0
Frequency	7	3	16	19	7	6

Average: 2.7

29) How important is the development of a library mission statement to other librarians at your institution? (Please circle the response that best reflects your opinion.)

	Very Important		Not Important			No Opinion
Rank	5	4	3	2	1	0
Frequency	4	3	14	18	11	8

Average: 2.4

30) How important is the development of a library mission statement to the teaching faculty at your institution? (Please circle the response that best reflects your opinion.)

	Very Important		Not Important			No Opinion
Rank	5	4	3	2	1	0
Frequency	0	1	9	20	18	10

Average: 1.9

31) How important is the development of a library mission statement to the administrators at your institution? (Please circle the response that best reflects your opinion.)

	Very Important		Not Important			No Opinion
Rank	5	4	3	2	1	0
Frequency	0	4	9	18	15	12

Average: 2.0

32) Additional comments:————————————————————————————
_____
_____
_____

Yes: 90; No: 42 Please check if you want a summary of the results.

Regional Accreditation Agency:

<u>32</u> Middle States Assocation   <u>18</u> New England Association

<u>45</u> North Central Association   <u>5</u> Northwest Association

<u>28</u> Southern Association   <u>4</u> Western Association

```
*******************************
*                             *
* Please enclose any sample   *
* mission or similar statements*
* from your library           *
*                             *
*******************************
```

Thank you for your
cooperation

Please Return To:

Larry Hardesty
Director of Library Services
Eckerd College Library
St. Petersburg, Florida 33733

5/22/85
LLH

1975 "Standards for College Libraries"

1975 STANDARDS FOR COLLEGE LIBRARIES

Standard 1:
Objectives of the Library

1   The college library shall develop an explicit statement of its objectives in accord with the goals and purposes of the college.

1.1   The development of library objectives shall be the responsibility of the library staff, in consultation with students, members of the teaching faculty, and administrative officers.

1.2   The statement of library objectives shall be reviewed periodically and revised as needed.

Commentary on Standard 1

The administration and faculty of every college have a responsibility to examine from time to time their education programs and to define the purposes and goals of the institution. Members of the library faculty share in this exercise, and they have thereafter the responsibility to promote library service consistent with institutional aims and methods. Successful fulfillment of this latter responsibility can best be attained when a clear and explicit statement of derivative library objectives is prepared and promulgated so that all members of the college community can understand and evaluate the appropriateness and effectiveness of library activities.

Preparation of library objectives is an obligation of the library faculty with the assistance of the rest of the library staff. In this effort, however, the library should seek in a formal or structured way the advice and guidance of students, of members of the teaching faculty, and of administrative officers. Library objectives should be kept current through periodic review and revision as needed.

In preparing its statement of objectives, the library staff should consider the evolution in the recent decades of new roles for the American college library. Although the college library continues as in the past to serve as the repository for the printed information needed by its patrons, its resources have now been enlarged through changes in the scope of the curriculum and by new concepts of instruction. Thus it now serves also as a complementary academic capability which affords to students the opportunity to augment their classroom experience with an independent avenue for learning beyond the course offerings of the institution. Even this instructional objective of the library, however, must be conceived and formulated within the overall academic purpose of the college.

Reprinted with permission from "Standards for College Libraries," College & Research Libraries 36 (October 1975): 278.

The Mission of the Undergraduate Library (Model Statement)

THE MISSION OF AN UNDERGRADUATE LIBRARY
(Model Statement)

Foreword

At the 1978 Midwinter Meeting of the ACRL Undergraduate Librarians Discussion Group (UGL), a group of librarians expressed interest in writing a model statement that would define the scope and articulate the UGL purpose in the academic library.

For the past year and a half the members of the group have met, corresponded, and worked on improving successive drafts of a mission statement. They have tried to address the key factors in the establishment of the UGL and develop a service philosophy that reflects the specific needs and the major components of an undergraduate library operation.

Librarians may use the model mission statement for comparison with their local statements, as evidence to support the purpose of the UGL, and as a starting point for continued definition and advocacy of the UGL at local and national levels. With these ends in mind, the study group has kept the text general. It has tried to provide distinctions unique to the UGL while encouraging breadth in interpretation to suit local situations.

The study group included Lan Dyson (Santa Cruz, California), Monty Maxwell (Bloomington, Indiana), Linda Phillips (Knoxville, Tennessee), Jay Poole (Austin, Texas), Tim Richards (Ann Arbor, Michigan), Liz Salzer (Stanford), Donna Senzig (Madison, Wisconsin) and Yorum Szekley (Cornell).

"The Mission of an Undergraduate Library" (Model Statement is here reprinted for the information of ACRL members).

The Mission of an Undergraduate Library (Model Statement)

The purpose of the undergraduate library is to take primary responsibility for meeting the library needs of undergraduate students in a large university environment. The nature of the environment, the specific needs of undergraduates, and the kinds of staff and services required to effectively meet those needs are more fully described in the following paragraphs.

Environment

The library systems of large universities generally consist of several major departmental libraries plus numerous special libraries and reading rooms spread over a large campus area. The materials collection of the library system is measured in millions of volumes. Each library within the system concentrates on the needs of the members of a specific department or field of study, and the quality of the library is defined in terms of the strengths of the research collection. Specialized services are often provided for those doing research, such as computerized searching of commercial resource data bases. The staff members of the libraries are selected for their ability to provide graduate-level reference services, to organize complex collections, and to select the often esoteric materials needed in a research library. In-depth subject knowledge and managerial skills are also frequently required.

Users

Into this research-oriented setting are placed large numbers of undergraduate students who come to the university with varying levels of experience and ability in using libraries. As a group most entering freshman share the following characteristics:

1. They do not yet have the sophisticated research skills needed during their college careers.
2. They are intimidated by the complexity and size of a large library system.
3. They are reluctant to ask for assistance in the use of a library.
4. They are unaware of the many services and resources which are available in university libraries.

The needs of academic library users are on a spectrum, with study space, instruction in basic research tools, and reserve books at one end, and primary source materials and special bibliographic services at the other end. All of the community may need something from anywhere on the spectrum: a faculty member may want to look at a basic work, and an occasional undergraduate may be writing a paper that requires access to archival materials. But the concentration of needs of the undergraduate is at one end of the spectrum, and the concentration of needs of the advanced graduate student or researcher is at the other end. It is at the former end of the spectrum that the undergraduate library focuses.

Information Services

An undergraduate library with a collection of the size and nature required to meet undergraduate needs is not easy to use. The identification of materials wanted is always confusing and often incomprehensible until the user is actually shown how the system works. Teaching students how to use a library is therefore a basic service provided by the staff of the undergraduate library. The teaching programs of undergraduate libraries are varied. They include teaching by personal contact and through the preparation of printed materials and audio-visual programs. They include formal library programs, team-teaching with instructors in their classes and/or classrooms, and informal, unstructured contacts with students. The programs generally include three types of activities reference and referral, orientation, and bibliographic instruction.

Reference encounters with undergraduates often result not only in answering specific questions, but also in personalized instruction in the methods of identifying and retrieving library materials. Supplemental to this personal contact is the provision of bibliographies, booklists, and other aids designed to introduce undergraduates to the materials available in the library and to guide them in finding materials. The reference service provided by undergraduate librarians is also a referral service. Referrals might assist an undergraduate in becoming aware of other campus and community libraries and information centers, as well as of personal supportive services, including academic, financial, health, and counseling services.

Orientation activities acquaint undergraduates with the facilities and services of the library. They include activities such as the distribution of maps and informational materials that describe the library system and the resources and services of the individual libraries within it, staff-conducted tours for groups, printed and audio-visual self-guided tours, and information desks. Orientation may also include public relations activities that help students become aware of the services and resources of the library.

Bibliographic instruction programs should improve ability of students to make effective use of the library collections, services, and staff and increase their ability to become independent library users. A wide range of programs may be offered including self-instructional point-of-use programs in the library, lectures to classes, workshops, term paper clinics, and for-credit courses in library research using workbooks, tests, and evaluations.

Reference service, bibliographic instruction, and orientation activities are appropriate for all levels and types of library users. The undergraduate librarian focuses on two problems that are particularly common to undergraduates—finding the materials they need, and knowing when to ask for help and having confidence to do so. Undergraduate libraries provide a laboratory in which to teach students how to use the library. The experience of using an undergraduate library is preparation for using all libraries, preparation not merely for graduate work and research, but also for learning to use information sources that will be needed by undergraduates for the rest of their lives as citizens, as consumers, in their professions, and for their recreational interests.

Collection

The subject scope of the undergraduate library will primarily support the teaching curriculum. A given undergraduate library would operate at one of the following collecting levels: (1) at the level of freshman and sophomore classes; (2) at all levels of undergraduate classwork; (3) at all levels except in those disciplines supported by specialized subject libraries, in which cases bibliographic support by the undergraduate library will be at the freshman and sophomore level. Since many undergraduate courses require large numbers of students to read the same library materials, direct curriculum support will be provided through reserve collections and through purchase of multiple copies of items with high demand.

The undergraduate library will provide not only the best materials of historical or research value (which might be duplicated in other libraries on campus) but also overviews of a subject jargon-free explanations of a field and introductory materials. Research reports and other items restricted to a very narrow subject area are less frequently of interest to undergraduates and will be purchased very selectively. The undergraduate library's collection of periodical reference material will concentrate on the more general periodical indexes, since these are most heavily used by undergraduates, the periodical collections should emphasize the titles covered by these indexes. Media collections in various audio-visual formats and ephemeral materials such as pamphlet and clipping files may also be provided as additional resources for effective undergraduate research.

Undergraduates select from a wide variety of courses and are therefore looking for library materials in order to meet course requirements. The subject range of the undergraduate library will be of sufficient comprehensiveness and depth so that, in general, the undergraduate will have a single starting point from which to find the basic information needed for papers, speeches, projects, etc. More advanced needs of undergraduates will be met by specific referral to graduate collections.

The information needs of undergraduates extend beyond the requirements of the curriculum. Undergraduate students are vitally interested in current events and in the current state of the world. The development of cultural and recreational interests is also an important part of the life of an individual, and the undergraduate years are a time of exploring the wide range of activities and opportunities available. The collections of the undergraduates should encourage them to seek materials in these areas. The collections of the undergraduate library will therefore be developed to meet these needs, since this is as important to undergraduate education and to the mission of the university as is the support of formal classroom instruction.

Staff

The staff members of the undergraduate library must have certain abilities in addition to their bibliographic and library skills. The ability to teach on a one-to-one basis is essential for all staff who interact with students. Undergraduate librarians need lecture and workshop skills if the instructional program of the library is to be successful. In addition, they should be able to interact with faculty in promoting effective use of library resources in relation to classroom activities. The ability to cooperate with staff of other libraries and resource centers is also needed.

Above all, the staff of an undergraduate library must have sympathy for undergraduates, an understanding of the pressures of campus life, and a concern for undergraduate needs and problems. Such sympathy will enable the library staff to treat undergraduates with respect, to make them feel comfortable in the library, and to encourage them to ask for help. Only this personal interaction with students will humanize their library contacts, open paths of communication for their growth in using libraries, and increase their respect for libraries.

Study Facilities

The environment of the undergraduate library should encourage the use of the library and its resources. The hours of operation must accommodate a range of student requirements based on class times, work commitments, and varied social habits. Many undergraduates live in environments which are not conducive to study; others simply prefer to study at the library. The undergraduate library should provide sufficient study spaces, based on the size of the student population, in a variety of seating to accommodate student needs and habits, e.g., quiet study of own materials, study with access to library resources, limited group study, and informal interaction.

Development

As undergraduate education changes, so must undergraduate library service. The undergraduate library must be innovative and experimental, alert to changing undergraduate needs, and must often adopt non-traditional library methodology. Current areas of development might include:

1. Continuing exploration of effective use of library materials (including audio-visual materials) in classroom teaching
2. Programs of bibliographic instruction
3. Service to special groups, e.g., the physically handicapped and visually impaired or the international student
4. Computer technology for use in creating bibliographic catalogs of library materials and for bibliographic searching of commercial data bases
5. Cooperative programs with other campus units, such as tutoring and counseling services

Developments in some of these areas may be at the library system level, rather than exclusively within the undergraduate library. However, it is the responsibility of the undergraduate library staff to shape these developments to meet the needs and problems of undergraduates.

Reprinted with permission from College & Research Libraries News 40 (November 1979): 317-319.

Mission Statements

Private Institutions (Under 2500 Students)

Albright College

LIBRARY

Mission

The mission of the Gingrich Library is to provide access to the print and nonprint records needed by the members of the College community for the successful pursuit of academic programs. It may, if appropriate, support non-academic programs by providing library resources and services.

The Library should afford students the opportunity to augment classroom experience with independent learning and encourage reading for recreation and general information.

The Library is responsible for assessing, cooperation with faculty and administration, college needs for library resources and services. It also seeks useful information, techniques and technology from the library, information, and education professions to meet needs and improve services. Finally, the Library develops users' skills in the full and effective use of library resources and services.

Goals

To develop a collection of print and nonprint records which meet the identified needs of its users.

To obtain records of the collections of other institutions or to provide access to the collections of other institutions when the library collection cannot itself meet the needs of its users.

To organize the collection for efficient retrieval of records by nationally approved conventions.

To provide a staff of qualified librarians and skilled support personnel to assist users in making appropriate and effective use of library collections, resources, facilities, and services.

To establish and maintain a range and quality of services which support, enhance, and promote the academic program of the college.

To acquire facilities of adequate size and quality to house the collections, resources, and services of the Library and to provide adequate space for users and library personnel.

To acquire financial support to meet Library needs.

To develop and maintain an audiovisual services program which enhances the instructional effectiveness of the faculty through the use of modern technology.

To offer instructional programs which develop library users' skills.

Review*

University of Albuquerque

I. A & B   Basic beliefs and purpose (mission)

The basic beliefs and purpose for the Library is summarized
in the mission statement of the Library:

"The Library should serve as a vital instrument for quality
education by enriching all parts of the educational process of
the University of Albuquerque. The Library should reflect and
support the mission of the University. The Library shares and
implements the school's aims and objectives. The Library
functions not as a separate entity, but is totally involved in
the teaching, learning process."

I. C   Basic functions

In carrying out its responsibilities in the academic program
effectively, the Library performs the following activities:

1. Selects library materials including books, periodicals, and
audio-visual software.
2. Prepares library materials for use by students, faculty and
others who require them. This would include classifying of
material, the cataloging of material, and the processing of
material (stamping, filing of catalog cards, labeling, etc.).
3. Circulates material from the general and reserve collection.
4. Provides reference service. This would include the answering
of questions; preparing bibliographies and reading lists;
and providing computer on-line searches.
5. Gives instruction on the use of the library through classroom
and individual instruction.
6. Interprets library services to the administration, faculty
and students.
7. Provides adequate and comfortable physical facilities for
studying including carrels, typing facilities, photocopying.
8. Provides inter-library loan services.
9. Makes available audio-visual services to the University
community.
10. Administers the total library program including the budget,
arrangement of various library activities, and public
relations activities.

CAPITAL UNIVERSITY LIBRARY

NORTH CENTRAL ASSOCIATION

SELF STUDY

I. Mission and Purpose

A. Purpose and Mission

1. Members of the University community pursuing both liberal and professional studies in their search for truth find in the library a means to meet their various information needs for learning and living.

2. Through the library's wide range of services and generous access to materials, the library's staff attempts to connect these many conceptual needs with the diverse and growing physical resources of the library.

B. Goals

1.1 The library will provide materials to fulfill the information needs of its constituency.

2.1 All students will know how to use Capital University Library—its collections and resources.

2.2 The library will provide prompt and efficient access to the materials in its collection.

2.3 The physical conditions of the library will be conducive to study and learning within an orderly but informal environment.

2.4 The library's staff will be adequate in size and sufficiently competent to achieve the library's mission.

C. Objectives

1.1.1 The library's acquisition system promptly and efficiently will acquire materials selected by faculty, students and librarians.

1.1.2 When appropriate, materials will be provided through interlibrary loan.

1.1.3 The library will participate in local resource sharing consortia as another means of providing materials and services.

1.1.4 The library's cataloging and processing system promptly and efficiently will process materials and make them available to users.

1.1.5 In building its collection the library will use standard reviewing media and such lists as Choice's outstanding books of the year, as well as other specialized bibliographies.

1.1.6 The library will maintain close liaison with faculty so as to keep abreast of their present and future library needs.

2.1.1 The library will provide a bibliographic instruction program with the potential for reaching all students.

2.2.2 The library will provide bibliographic access to its materials by way of a modern and efficient cataloging system.

2.2.3 The library will provide physical access to its materials by way of an efficient circulation and reserve system.

2.2.4 The library will provide assistance in the use of its materials by way of a professional and clerical staff that provides ready reference and catalog assistance services.

2.2.5 The library will maintain a publications program that informs faculty and students of the library's collections and services.

2.2.6 The library will maintain a security system to protect the integrity of its collections.

2.3.1 The library will provide sufficient and varied seating for its constituency.

2.3.2 The library will provide a variety of study areas appropriate to use of the various kinds of materials in the collection.

2.3.3 The physical environment of the library will be conducive to study and research.

2.3.4 The library will provide space for an exhibit series.

2.4.1 High standards for recruitment of professional and clerical staff will be maintained.

2.4.2 Opportunities for professional growth and enrichment will be provided for the staff.

Carleton College

STATEMENT OF PURPOSE AND

GENERAL COLLECTION MANAGEMENT GUIDELINES

FOR THE CARLETON COLLEGE LIBRARY

The mission of Carleton College is to create a complementary and supportive, demanding environment in which students can pursue their education, and where they can test their interests and abilities and develop a capacity to make informed, responsible judgments with respect to themselves, and the world around them. The purpose of the library is to support this mission by facilitating the interaction between users of information and recorded knowledge to the degree possible within human and economic limitations. To promote this interaction, facilities, materials, and services of a quality commensurate with that of the academic program are required. The curriculum should be the primary criterion for determining the focus of the library in molding these components, if we acknowledge that the focus of the college is on the teaching of undergraduate students and that this focus will not change in forseeable future.

The library must provide an atmosphere that promotes study, encourages scholarly pursuits, and fosters the academic excellence that is the primary goal of the College. It does this by maintaining physical space where individuals and small groups can comfortably engage in formal scholarly activities or in the serendipitous pursuit of knowledge that a good library will engender. Space must also be provided, along with necessary furnishings and equipment, for the convenient storage, retrieval, and use of recorded knowledge in whatever form may be required by the curriculum, and to the degree feasible, by the research and other interests of the community.

It is the responsibility of the library to maintain a quality collection of materials that furthers the purpose and mission of the institution as a whole in meeting the needs of the undergraduate student. The primary emphasis should be on those materials likely to be used by faculty in preparing their courses and by students in doing research related to their studies. Faculty scholarship in the College is, of course, essential, and it is a secondary mission of the library to facilitate this by providing the basic materials faculty need to carry on research to the degree possible within the limited resources available. However, the intensive collecting of materials that are unlikely to be used by students in order to support faculty research, or the building of highly specialized resources to support advanced studies that will never be part of the Carleton curriculum are outside the scope of the library program at Carleton for the following reasons:

It is far less costly to send faculty to major research collections than to attempt to duplicate and maintain such collections here.

28

Faculty needs are usually more long-term and allow for better planning than those of students.

Faculty have greater access to other collections, interlibrary loan, and similar forms of resource sharing than do students.

There is no agenda to develop graduate programs, to grow into a university or to change the basic focus of the college to anything other than its undergraduate program.

The library must provide services to its users that are designed to facilitate the identification, location, delivery, and use of recorded knowledge. If the curriculum determines the focus of the library, then these services need to be integrated into the teaching and research fiber of the College. This can be accomplished only through an active and continuing dialogue between faculty, library staff, and students that has as its goal the development of maximum facility in the use of recorded knowledge by students. This is consistent with the goal of the College to prepare students for lifelong growth and continuing education. The service functions of the library include the following:

Maintain library materials in an easily accessible, logical, and orderly arrangement that conforms to accepted standards and best meets the needs of all users of the library, and also, manage the distribution, use, and retrieval of library materials while providing for their protection and preservation.

Identify, through encouraging, facilitating, and coordinating the active participation of the faculty, the bibliographical and other resources needed to support present and anticipated curricula and to develop and manage outstanding undergraduate collections in the subject fields emphasized at Carleton, and also, maintain a general library collection suited to the interests and needs of an educated person as represented by a Carleton undergraduate.

Prepare clear, accurate records in accordance with standards generally accepted by academic libraries in whatever formats, consistent with reasonable cost, best facilitate the work of users in identifying materials pertinent to their needs, make it possible for us to participate in resource sharing arrangements with others, and expedite the internal operations of the library.

Provide assistance to users in the manipulation and interpretation of bibliographical records to identify, locate, and efficiently utilize library materials and information from any source that is pertinent to their research, study, or other interests.

Develop, in conjunction with faculty, instructional programs and other aids to the use of the library and its resources that are designed to help students make the most efficient and productive use of their time, develop skills that will enhance their ability to independently utilize this and other libraries, and gain maximum benefit from our investment in the library.

Arrange easy access to materials that the library does not own by negotiating and maintaining cooperative arrangements with other institutions, utilizing cost-effective means of rapidly identifying, locating, and obtaining needed materials within current legal restrictions on the use of borrowed materials, and facilitate the use of borrowed materials within the community.

Manage the business of the library efficiently according to established principles of library management and in accordance with College policy, and also, gather, review, and evaluate information on the procedures, programs, and policies of the library in order to seek means of improving its effectiveness.

Keep abreast of the needs of Carleton library users and of new trends and technologies that facilitate library operations and services, and keep the community of users and the library staff can work cooperatively to maintain library policies and services that make the most efficient use of available resources to meet the needs of all users.

Foster cultural awareness and appreciation of the book and other library materials as aesthetic entities by creating displays, etc., and also, seek out aspects of the collections that might be utilized or developed to provide a feeling of uniqueness to the library.

The degree to which the library is fulfilling its stated purpose can be measured by the degree to which its three basic components—facilities, materials, and services—are reflective of, and relevant to the academic program of the College as expressed by its curriculum.

Denison University

William Howard Doane Library
General Operation Policy
Fall 1980

The William Howard Doane Library is maintained to support the educational mission of Denison University by 1) providing library materials, 2) providing library patrons with assistance and training in the efficient use of information resources, and 3) providing library patrons with space and facilities for inhouse use of library materials.

The library's regular patrons are Denison students, Denison faculty and supportive staff members and their families, and adult residents of Granville. Direct borrowing privileges are also available to individuals who can identify themselves as students or faculty members of other institutions of higher education. Special borrowing privileges can be arranged for individuals not in the above categories at the discretion of the library staff and, ultimately, the library director. Inhouse use of materials is open to all.

Financial support for library operations comes primarily from funds allocated by the University for library purposes. In addition, the library accepts financial gifts, endowed or unendowed, to supplement the acquisitions budget; gifts for this purpose may be either unrestricted or designated for use in prescribed subject areas. Gifts of library materials can be accepted if they, and the conditions of the gift, are appropriate to the collection.

Collection

The library acquires, processes, and houses those library materials, in whatever format*, which the faculty feels are essential to the successful pursuit of undergraduate studies in the various disciplines offered at the University. In addition, as funds and space allow, the library acquires, processes, and houses 1) materials of general interest to an educated public and 2) materials in support of faculty research and professional development.

Though prime responsibility for the selection of library materials in the subject fields lies with the faculty, the library staff supplements faculty ordering, with particular emphasis upon reference and bibliographic works. Decision on the appropriateness to the collection of any item, whether recommended for purchase or received as a gift, is normally made by the library director. Should a department or donor challenge the director's decision, the dispute shall be turned over to the Dean of the College for final settlement.

Size of the collection is determined by rate of acquisition and an ongoing weeding program. Departments have a continuing responsibility for

---

*Audio-visual materials, except for phonodiscs, phonodisc listening facilities, micromedia materials, and micromedia readers, are the responsibility of the Media Services Center.

recommending withdrawal of obsolete library materials. When a shelving area of the library becomes full, the library director, in consultation with the concerned departments, will select materials for storage. Materials in storage will be available to library patrons on a call basis. When the storage area is full, the concerned departments and other interested faculty members will be asked to select materials for disposal. Such selection will be based principally upon the history of use of a book or journal, but the following matters will also be considered:

> the work's uniqueness in the collection;
> reputation of the work in its field;
> need for duplicates of a title;
> strength of the collection in the field to which a
>   work belongs;
> inclusion of a title in published indexes.

Before final disposal the entire faculty will be given the opportunity to review titles selected for discard.

Lost or missing books will normally not be replaced until at least one year after the loss is discovered. Missing issues of journals are replaced, whenever possible, when the volume is due for binding. Missing journal volumes are replaced, whenever possible, on a need basis only, but usually not before a year after the loss is discovered.

Services

The public service function of the library is designed to assist patrons in obtaining needed information, wherever that information may be located, and in whatever format. The local collection is maintained as the prime information source for library patrons, but the library staff will help patrons obtain access to other sources in instances when our collection does not meet the patrons' information needs. Locating proper sources of information is part of the library's service function; to fulfill this obligation, a trained, professional reference librarian is regularly on duty to assist in searches of the reference collection, the bibliographic collection, the general collection, the government document collection, and whatever bibliographic information is available to us through computers.

Materials in the collection are made available to library patrons through established, announced circulation procedures. Materials needed for specific courses can be maintained in a limited circulation reserve collection on a semester to semester basis. Items not held in this library can usually be obtained through interlibrary loan within one to three weeks. This library also maintains direct borrowing arrangements with various other institutions and will assist patrons in their efforts to use materials from other libraries.

Training

The development of competence in obtaining needed information is an integral part of a Denison education; fostering such competence is a principal responsibility of the library staff. An up-to-date handbook for this library is always available, and January Term courses in library operations and librarian assisted independent study are offered. The reference staff, in consort with members of the teaching faculty, devises and carries out library instruction tailored to course work and also assists individual patrons in developing information finding skills. Faculty cooperation is sought in making students understand how important these skills are and providing valid contexts in which they can be developed.

Facilities

Within the limits of the architectural space available, the library endeavors to provide the easiest possible access to the collection and a comfortable atmosphere conducive to scholarly work. The collection is shelved as systematically as space allows, and the traditional locating tools - card catalog, periodical indexes, bibliographic and reference works - are all located as close together as possible. Through Denison membership in OCLC, Inc., the library is in the mainstream of current technological development in the field and will make every effort to provide the most up-to-date procedures for information search and retrieval, so that Denison students not only have access to the information, but also have the opportunity to acquire the information-gathering skills that new library technology will demand of them in the future.

Eckerd College

STATEMENT OF PURPOSES OF THE ECKERD
COLLEGE LIBRARY

Preface

Certain assumptions about the role of the library in the academic
environment underlie the promulgation of this "Statement of Purposes of
the Eckerd College Library". They may be briefly described as follows:

1) The library is of paramount importance to students and faculty
in fulfilling the educational mission of the institution. The
centrality of the library to the educational mission must be
understood and supported by those responsible for allocation of
instructional resources.

2) The library should reveal the general scope of the learned and
creative world and foster broad interests among its users. The
extent of the library's holdings must be reasonable proportion
to the needs served.

3) The librarians and classroom instructors need to work closely
together in planning the development and employment of the
library to achieve their educational objectives.

4) The librarians should be active participants in teaching and
learning, not merely custodians of books and other materials.
They must demonstrate their competence using criteria
comparable to other faculty and staff, and be given sufficient
responsibility and funds to facilitate optimum functioning.

5) The physical surroundings of the library must be conducive to
use. Factors such as shelving, seating, lighting, and arrangement of materials must be judged on the basis of their
serviceability in making the library a comfortable place for
study. Nothing else matters much if the facilities are not used.[1]

This "Statement of Purposes of the Eckerd College Library" is written
with an understanding of and appreciation for the special and particular
aims of Eckerd College. These aims are described in the "Mission and
Objectives" statement of Eckerd College, adopted by the Board of
Trustees on February 21, 1978. Broadly stated, Eckerd College is a
"free-standing, coeducational college of liberal arts and sciences, related
by covenant" to the Presbyterian College, U.S.A., serving primarily an
undergraduate clientele.

As an undergraduate instructional institution, Eckerd College seeks
to provide students with a broad understanding of the human experience
while encouraging them to explore at least one discipline in some depth.
There exists a strong commitment to general education beginning with
the Western Heritage sequence in the first year and culminating in the
Judeo-Christian perspective and an issues-oriented seminar in the senior
year.

As a church-related institution, the College asks each student to examine values as well as facts. Through a commitment to the primary importance of teaching, the faculty provide personal attention to students in their individual development through such innovative programs as Autumn Term and the Mentorship program. Students are guided in developing an appreciation of how new knowledge is created and evaluated from various perspectives without becoming too narrowly focused early in their academic career. In addition, they are asked to examine the interrelatedness of the various disciplines and to integrate the liberal arts and career preparation. Through a unique combination of various academic programs, Eckerd College provides an opportunity for students to develop a broad, humane perspective on the human experience.

This statement has been developed so that available resources can be focused on those policies, practices, and procedures that best enable the Eckerd College Library to support the Mission of the College. In addition, through preparation and promulgation of this statement, the College community will better understand and evaluate the appropriateness and effectiveness of the Library's policies, practices, and procedures.

Statement of Purposes

The Eckerd College Library exists primarily to support the educational aims of the College, and it does so in a variety of ways. In general, the Library assists the faculty and other members of the College community in the selection and use of that portion of the human record that relates to and furthers the educational mission of the College. The library has the primary responsibility for the acquisition, organization, and maintenance of these materials so that they will be readily available to all members of the College community.

Among the major responsibilities of the Library, the most important is the assistance provided in the selection of those materials that will support the aims of the College. Given the limited resources available and the finite aims of the College, priority should be placed on selection of general instructional materials that directly support the undergraduate curriculum. Working together, librarians and classroom instructors should emphasize the selection of the materials that will be used either by students in their undergraduate studies or by classroom instructors in preparation for their undergraduate teaching.

Materials selected for the Library should reflect the experiences of a broad range of subjects, periods, and cultures to enable students to understand the breadth and depth of human experience. The Library must provide an appropriate sampling of recorded knowledge to allow students to develop an understanding of the human experience as encompassed by the liberal arts and sciences. Available materials should offer students the opportunity to encounter and evaluate alternative viewpoints to free themselves from provincialism and prejudice. Finally, the Library should provide sufficient resources so that students can develop an understanding of how recorded knowledge is organized and structured. It is through such an understanding that they can become self-directed, lifelong learners in the liberal arts tradition.

In light of this College's commitment to the primary importance of teaching, priority should be placed on the acquisition of the library materials that support undergraduate education. Nonetheless, members of the faculty are expected to engage in research as well as other professional activities, and the staff of the Eckerd College Library is committed to supporting the faculty in these endeavors. Typically, this involves the acquisition of books and periodical subscriptions such that the Library is in conformity with professional library standards for liberal arts institutions of the first rank. However, the extensive acquisition of expensive research materials in highly specialized areas should be undertaken only upon careful consideration of resources available to support undergraduate education.

In addition to permanent acquisition of materials, research activity is supported through interlibrary loan and cooperative lending agreements with other institutions. Access to materials contained in outside collections is obtained through major indexing and abstracting sources available either in papercopy or through online computer databases.

While interlibrary loan and other cooperative agreements may provide some materials needed by the College community, the Library must receive adequate support from the institution to insure that it will be the primary resource for the library-related needs of the College community. Materials for which there are legitimate recurring needs should be purchased by the Library.

Within the Library, there should be a proper balance among the resources so that the Library can best achieve its purpose. The library director has primary responsibility for the allocation of resources within this budget. The library director, acting in consultation with the faculty library committee and the other librarians, will determine the procedure for the expenditures of this budget. In particular, the faculty library committee should be consulted closely in the allocation of the book and periodical budget.

In addition, the entire Eckerd College community shares a responsibility for the realization of the full potential of the Library. Specifically, the classroom faculty and librarians have a mutual responsibility to consult carefully with each other in the areas of book and periodical fund allocations and selections, permanent removal from the Library of books and periodicals, and discontinuation of standing orders and periodical subscriptions. Besides the selection and maintenance of library materials, the classroom faculty and librarians have a responsibility to cooperate to insure appropriate use of these materials.

Decision making in these areas should take into consideration such factors as the mission of Eckerd College, funds available to the Library, expertise and time of the librarians and library staff, utilization of library materials, and available library space. Necessary cooperation and consultation can be conducted through a variety of methods, such as meetings between library and classroom faculty, communications through the library newsletter, and meetings of the library director with the faculty library committee.

As an undergraduate instructional library, the Eckerd College Library should place more emphasis on careful selection and use of materials than on comprehensiveness and preservation of materials. A major responsibility of librarians is to promote and assist in the effective use of materials selected and acquired. Librarians and classroom instructors should work closely together to encourage students to make sophisticated and meaningful use of available library resources. Undergraduate students should develop the ability not only to retrieve information, but also to evaluate and synthesize it. Such skills are necessary in a complex and changing world. Individual and group instruction in the intricacies of the Library, closely integrated with regular course assignments, are important vehicles through which this purpose may be fulfilled. As is the case in other areas of the College, the Library should be committed to fostering the individual development of each student.

Policies, procedures, and practices related to the acquisition, organization, and maintenance of the library materials are primarily the responsibility of the library staff. In particular, these policies, procedures, and practices should support the major purposes of the Library relating to the selection and use of library materials. Once selected, materials should be promptly acquired and placed in the Library collection. The materials should be organized and made available so as to encourage their use by library patrons. Application of acceptable classification and cataloging principles and the maintenance of extensive library hours are two of the methods through which the Library should encourage use of its collections.

Circulation and security systems must provide for both reasonable use of materials by individuals and the availability of these materials to other members of the College community who might wish to use them. The Library is the primary vehicle through which books, periodicals, and related materials are purchased for wide use of the College community. These materials should be recognized as property of Eckerd College with the library staff given the responsibility for their maintenance and organization. Extensive circulation periods to individual patrons that may effectively result in loss of ownership of these materials as well as overly restrictive circulation periods that unnecessarily deprive patrons access to the materials should be avoided.

Each item in the library collection should justify its continued existence in the Library in relation to the aims and resources of the College. As materials should be selected carefully for addition to the Library, materials also should be selected carefully for removal from the Library. As ideas become outdated and no longer useful, so do their containers. Library materials should be monitored regularly to determine those that no longer serve a useful purpose at Eckerd College and may be withdrawn.

In addition to providing intellectual and creative resources, the Library should offer an attractive and comfortable environment that encourages use. This includes provisions for group as well as individual study, adequate lighting and environmental control (heating and air-conditioning), and a variety of seating, such as individual carrels, lounge furniture, and group seating, that reflects the variety of needs of library users. The seating and shelving capacity of the Library should be developed to meet the recognized standards of college libraries in relation to the enrollment of Eckerd College and the size of the collection of the Library. Since the Library is a major facility where students are to contemplate their studies and a frequent focal point for visitors to the College, it should be kept visually attractive through proper maintenance and periodic refurbishment. Sufficient funds should be allocated to the Library by the College to insure that these basic requirements are met.

Given the size and resources of the College, the Library can best achieve its purpose in one central facility. While a small portion of library materials may be convenient to a few members of the academic community when situated in outlying locations, these materials are less available for the rest of the academic community. The materials in outlying collections are seldom available for the same number of hours or as well-organized as materials in the main library. Such collections also usually result in additional costs in the form of added staff and duplicate materials.

This "Statement of Purposes of the Eckerd College Library" should be viewed as a document subject to monitoring and revision. As aims of Eckerd College change and new programs are created and old programs are discontinued, this document should reflect those changes. This document should not serve to restrict nor limit the development of the Library, but, instead, it should be used to better understand and evaluate the policies, procedures, and practices of the Library given the aims and resources of both the Library and Eckerd College.

[1] Adopted from Characteristics of Excellence in Higher Education, Commission on Higher Education of the Middle States Association of Colleges and Schools, 1982.

4/15/85

Up̀john Library
Kalamazoo College

Statement of Goals and Objectives

Mission

The mission of the Up̀john Library is to provide services and resources to meet the present and future scholarly and informational needs of the Kalamazoo College community, and in so far as possible, to share these resources with the broader scholarly community.

Continuing Goals

1. To provide a collection of information resources which meet most of the curricular, informational, and research needs of the College community.

2. To organize and control the collection for maximum utilization.

3. To maintain the collection in usable physical condition and conserve the material for future generations of users.

4. To organize, monitor, and evaluate library services and procedures to assure the effective and efficient utilization of funds available now and in the future.

5. To provide bibliographic aids and assistance in identifying, locating, and using information resources including those not available in the Kalamazoo College collections, but which are needed to support the instructional and research programs of the College.

6. To provide facilities and equipment for the storage and use of information resources.

7. To maintain and further develop a highly capable library staff through systematic programs of career development and effective utilization of individual talents to fulfill the library's mission and support its objectives.

8. To maintain effective administrative planning services.

9. To maintain a close and meaningful working relationship with administrative and academic departments, academic planning groups, and the user communities, to assure effective development of library services consistent with objectives and programs of the College, and to advise the College as to requirements and costs of these resources.

10. To promote the use of the library and information resources.

11. To continually investigate opportunities to increase services and access to collections beyond the College through cooperative programs with other libraries, library organizations, and information retrieval systems.

12. To maintain constant exploration of professional and technological developments with a constant view to applicability for Kalamazoo College.

13. To insure continued development and utilization of those collections of a specialized or pre-eminent nature which are distinctive to Kalamazoo College and which are of regional and national interest.

Lake Forest College

Mission and Goals

Mission statement:

To contribute to the liberal arts education of the student body:

— in the development of intellectual and academic independence through reading and research and

— in providing a range of expertise, experience and stimuli complementary to classroom instruction.

Goals

1. To meet the research demands of the teaching program through:

    - development and maintenance of collections which are tailored to programs;
    - use of outside collections for backup (inter-library loan, visits to other libraries nearby);
    - interpretive services (reference, bibliographic instruction, data base searching) to assist researchers (student and faculty) in using the collections.

2. To meet demands for direct support of instructional effort through:

    - effective reserve loan operations;
    - audio-visual services;
    - facilities for study, including group study room for library-related activities;
    - provision of reliable photocopy service.

3. To meet the research demands of faculty, whose own growth and development nourishes the vital core of the College.

4. To stimulate research demand through introduction of services which facilitate access and open new teaching and research dimensions:

    - new compute links;
    - bibliographic instruction to bridge the gap between faculty expectation and student preparation in complex research areas.

5. To meet reasonable demands on library resources from the community and from other libraries, as a participant in resource-sharing activities.

6. To develop facilities and programs to meet student entertainment/leisure needs.

    - books and magazines for recreational reading set up in a

41

comfortable Browsing Section, perhaps where the Treasure Room is currently located;
- audio-visual materials and a properly-equipped area in which they could be used.

7. To serve as one measure of the quality of the College, through community relations about library activities and collections.

3. Major Policies and Objectives

   a. Commitment to resource sharing, keyed by our location (the resource-rich Chicago region and the public policy leadership of Illinois).

   b. Close library/faculty cooperation for innovation.

   c. Use of student workers.

   d. Coverage of a broad range of services.

   e. Active involvement in the implementation of automated library services as a means to solving library problems.

   f. Partial depository for government documents.

   g. Microforms are an integral part of our core collection.

   h. Commitment to having — and developing (in some cases) — our special collections.

   i. Acceptance of gift materials, and acquisition of retrospective collections to enhance our collections.

   j. Reliance on faculty for book selection; the selection policy is essentially curriculum-based.

   k. Use of grant funds to address key library issues and needs.

   l. Provision of direct lending, reference, and library-access services to non-campus users: Lake Forest community, LIBRAS college students and faculty (including Barat), and others.

Lewis & Clark College

I. Goals

    A. Aubrey R. Watzek Library Statement of Purpose and Goals 1975

        1) To support and to further the purposes and goals of the College as an educational institution.

        2) To provide, to the extent necessary and in the variety possible, material, service and equipment needed for purposes:

            a) To support the instructional program,
            b) To aid faculty research,
            c) To encourage student exploration and study outside of curricular offerings,
            d) To supply reading experiences by which the student may be encouraged to form the habit of self-education and to see the library as the principal facility for the self-education.

        3) To enable the student and faculty member through personal reference assistance to locate information and material which can be found in indexes, catalogs, bibliographies and reference books.

        4) To instruct students in the use of the library and its collections, its possibilities in learning and teaching, to provide familiarizing experiences with the major bibliographic resources in their fields, and in research methods.

        5) To assure physical facilities that are suitable in lighting, ventilation, comfort, variety of furnishings, and quality of environment to assure the best possible conditions for use of materials and equipment.

        6) To provide an archival depository for the correspondence, records, publications and other materials derived from ongoing work of the College.

Wheaton College

Madeleine Clark Wallace Library
Norton, Massachusetts

Mission of the College:

"The objective for which the Wheaton College Corporation exists shall be the education of women."

From the Statutes of Wheaton College, February, 1978

Mission of the Library:

The mission of the Wheaton College Library is to support and enhance the activities of the College by serving the curricular and information needs of its students, faculty and staff.

Goals of the Library:

1. To develop a balanced collection of materials.

2. To encourage library use.

3. To assist patrons in gaining access to library collections and other resources.

4. To collect and maintain the historical records of the institution.

5. To provide and maintain a comfortable and stimulating physical facility.

6. To improve library services continuously.

7. To support the Library Bill of Rights of the American Library Association.

8. To facilitate Library staff participation in continuing education and professional opportunities.

9. To inform the Wheaton Community of current developments in library and information science.

10/84

44

Private Institutions (2500 Students And Over)

Bucknell University

MISSION, GOALS, AND OBJECTIVES

ELLEN CLARKE BERTRAND LIBRARY

MISSION

    The mission of the Bertrand Library shall reflect and
support the mission of the University. Bertrand Library shall
assure both bibliographical and physical access to the body of
recorded knowledge and information needed to support the
instructional programs, research efforts, and social
responsibilities of the University.

Revised 5/84

46

INFORMATION RESOURCES GOAL

The resources of the Library shall support the curricula of the University, provide the basis for a well-rounded liberal education and, to the extent possible, meet the research needs of the University community.

OBJECTIVES

1. Identify and constantly monitor user needs.

2. Identify, select and acquire Library materials, including books, periodicals, documents, etc. in a timely manner.

3. Obtain access to or acquire sources of information regardless of formats in a timely manner.

4. On a continuing basis evaluate and redefine the collection and other information resources.

INFORMATION ACCESS GOAL

The Library shall provide bibliographic access to resources in all formats within the University as well as to such material outside the University by means of interlibrary loan, computer networks, etc.

OBJECTIVES

1. Acquire or access retrospective bibliographies and current bibliographies and indexes, regardless of format, to provide maximum access to information both within and beyond the University.

2. Provide timely interlibrary loan service to meet informational needs of the University community which cannot be met by the Library's collection.

3. Catalog and process materials with speed, accuracy, and economy.

4. Provide and maintain on-line access to the collection.

5. Maintain good physical access to the Library collection.

FREEDOM OF INFORMATION GOAL

Resources shall not be excluded from the Library because of the origin, background or views of those contributing to their creation. Books and other Library resources shall be available for the interest, information and enlightenment of all Library users, which are primarily faculty and students but which also include the wider community.

INSTRUCTION GOAL

The Library staff shall insure, through as many instruction programs and services as possible, that all students and other members of the University community become competent Library and information users.

OBJECTIVES

1. Establish and monitor competence in Library use.

2. Determine method most likely to assure, on a University-wide basis, competence in Library and information skills.

3. Establish programs of instruction for various audiences.

CONSERVATION GOAL

The Library shall maintain the collection in the best possible physical condition.

OBJECTIVES

1. Establish or define standards for good physical condition of the entire Library collection.

2. Maintain established standards while continuously reviewing current methods and exploring new methods for appropriate conservation of materials.

COMMUNICATION GOAL

Open and effective communication within the University community, within the Library and with other libraries is essential. Use and understanding of the Library's resources and information services and their further development consistent with the University's goals shall be encouraged. To this end, constructive working relationships with academic departments, the student body and other units of the University shall be fostered.

OBJECTIVES

1. Make our users, including but not limited to faculty, students and administration aware of materials and services available.

2. Maintain awareness of developments within the University community which may have implications for the Library.

3. Maintain awareness within Library staff of their responsibility to communicate what is happening within the Library to each other.

4. Maintain contacts with other administrative units within the University and seek opportunities to represent the Library on University committees and policy-formation groups.

5. Maintain professional contacts with individuals and organizations on a local, regional, and national level.

6. Provide opportunity for Library staff to enhance their

communication skills.

7. Explore new methods of communication.

FACILITIES GOAL

The Library shall provide physical facilities and equipment which meet the needs of users for convenient access to information and of staff for an accommodating work environment. Inviting surroundings which encourage study and which establish an atmosphere which is conducive to productive use shall be created. An appropriate environment for the conservation of materials will be maintained.

OBJECTIVES

1. Plan for and seek out appropriate equipment, furniture, and new technology to improve study space, staff working conditions, and work flow.

2. Assure materials and services are easily located.

3. Define and maintain environmnental standards.

4. Review space needs and plan for changing circumstances on an ongoing basis.

STAFF GOAL

The Library shall recruit, train, and develop personnel possessing the wide range of knowledge, skills and experience necessary to meet the diverse Library service requirements of the University community.

OBJECTIVES

1. Establish long-range staffing plan.

2. Recruit widely and hire selectively in accordance with Equal Opportunity Affirmative Action guidelines of the University.

3. Establish training and orientation program for new Library staff.

4. Maintain performance appraisal system.

5. Provide developmental experiences for the entire staff.

6. Support efforts to establish and maintain an equitable compensation plan for all levels of Library staff.

7. Establish systems for recruitment, training, and evaluation of student assistants.

LIBRARY ORGANIZATION GOAL

The organization of the entire staff shall be flexible enough to meet changing needs, such as new curricular demands and the new technologies of information access and its dissemination. The staff shall be organized in a way that permits easy and rapid communication for the interchange of ideas, both within the Library and outside the Library, and for the coordination of its various functions and timely achievement of goals.

OBJECTIVES

1. Continuously review Library policies and procedures.

2. Continuously review Library organization to determine if it provides optimum framework for service to our users.

FINANCIAL RESOURCES.

In cooperation with appropriate University departments, sources of funding, both within the University and outside, snall be identified and secured. Financial resources shall be expended judiciously for the greatest benefit of the University community.

OBJECTIVES

1. Ensure that the Library budget is adequate to provide materials and services.

2. Establish internal Library planning cycle coordinated with University budget process to review needs of current programs and needs of potential new programs.

3. Monitor accounting procedures and expenditure of funds so that Library remains within budget.

4. Work with University Relations to obtain outside funding for special projects and needs.

5. With University Relations establish and maintain contacts with potential donors.

Butler University

May, 1984

Mission and Goals of the Irwin Library System

Mission

It is the mission of the Irwin Library System to provide the library resources and services required to support the goals of Butler University.

Guiding Principles

1. To recognize that the Irwin Library System is a part of, and must operate within, the larger organizational framework of Butler University.

2. To support the University commitment to concerns beyond the institution proper.

3. To participate in inter-library cooperation that enhances the quality of learning resources available for research and study for both ourselves and other institutions who agree with the spirit of shared information while at the same time making the most efficient use of available financial and human resources.

4. To view the library as a dynamic system requiring continuous evaluation and adjustment in order to provide the flexibility to accommodate changing environmental and patron demands.

5. To strive for the highest possible organizational effectiveness in order to best utilize material and human resources.

6. To aim for a harmonious internal working environment that will produce personal satisfaction and achieve Library System goals.

7. To resist attempts to censor information.

8. To respect patrons' rights and to guard their privacy.

9. To acquire and preserve recorded knowledge needed to support the mission of the University as well as provide the tools to support access to this knowledge for teaching and research.

10. To maintain flexibility in meeting patron needs, whether planning services, applying regulations, interpreting policy, or providing resources.

11. To provide the maximum possible access to information and use of the the collections so that the greatest number of patrons can be satisfied, yet recognizing the unique needs of some individuals.

12. To recognize that patron service is the ultimate goal of all Library System activities.

Goals

The basic objective of the Irwin Library System is to facilitate access to information, library materials, and services for members of the University community through the common endeavor of the entire staff to acquire, process, service, and preserve library materials. In order to achieve this basic objective, the library staff must strive to:

1. Develop the collection, both current and retrospective, based upon a thorough knowledge of the instructional and research needs of the University.

2. Develop and establish more effective collection control through improved circulation service, increased security, and collection preservation, including proper attention to materials requiring special considerations.

3. Study and provide means for improving access to library materials and information through staff awareness and development, user education, and the utilization of expanded library services.

4. Improve and expedite the processing of library materials through both innovative and traditional methods to provide necessary bibliographic control and access.

5. Continue to study, ascertain, and appraise the library's responsibilities and ability to serve others beyond the University community.

6. Develop cooperative programs for resource sharing to meet the needs of the University community and to share these resources with other libraries, researchers, and scholars.

7. Systematically examine space problems and needs to ascertain the best possible arrangement of materials, services, and staff for maximum effectiveness and efficiency in library operations.

8. Maintain and develop a highly capable library staff through systematic programs of recruitment, career development, and effective utilization of individual talents.

9. Establish and maintain an effective liaison between the library staff and it's primary clientele in order to assist in the planning and development of library programs and services to meet the changing needs of the University.

10. Utilize the widest possible number of avenues of communication, both

- 59 -

internally and externally, to insure the clearest understanding of library policies and programs.

11. Continue to review the above goals and develop new goals as appropriate.

Everett Needham Case Library
COLGATE UNIVERSITY
HAMILTON, NEW YORK 13346

(315) 824-1000

MISSION STATEMENT

The mission of Colgate University is:

> ...to provide a superior undergraduate educational ex-
> perience in the liberal arts which will be relevant to
> contemporary issues of society and will help qualified
> students prepare themselves for moral, intellectual,
> social, and aesthetic self-fulfillment and leadership.*

Within this institutional framework, it is the mission of the University
Library to provide those information resources and services which are necessary
to support the Colgate undergraduate experience and to help students gain that
command of the varieties of information resource which is vital to life-long
self-fulfillment and leadership.

In operational terms, it is the mission of the University Library to
provide access to that recorded knowledge which the university community requires in the pursuit of its mission. This access places on the library three
requirements. It requires the selection, acquisition, organization, description, and preservation of appropriate materials within the library and the
maximization of the library's users' access to resources only available elsewhere. It requires facilitating the identification and communication of knowledge via instruction in the organization and use of libraries, electronic
data bases, and other information sources as well as in the bibliography of
the various disciplines. It requires the maintenance of the proper environment for the study and use of knowledge recorded in many formats.

draft
12/80
revised
12/18/80

* Source: The Masterplan of Colgate University. 1980. p.2

Creighton University   ALUMNI LIBRARY
                             Mission≈
                        Goals - Objectives

The intellectual and the esthetic growth of the student are two of
the stated objectives of Creighton as a university. The Alumni
Library of the university is in a unique position to contribute
towards both of these objectives. As the Alumni Library works
towards the university's established objectives, the library must
form its own set of objectives and its own mission statement.

Mission Statement

The Alumni Library as a major educational and cultural resource
center provides the materials essential for Creighton University
students to complete course requirements and assignments and to
furnish informational resources to support student and faculty research.
Further, the Alumni Library offers to students, but to a lesser degree,
non-course oriented materials for their leisure and/or their esthetic
development.

     To fulfill its mission, the library must establish certain goals,
goals that are practical yet visionary, that are founded in good educational philosophy and that have both the understanding and the commitment of the total university. Therefore, this mission statement will
enumerate the library's goals and specify the objectives to reach them.
It is an automatic assumption that goals are less likely to change, but
that new objectives and specific tasks will replace present objectives
and tasks as they are met or are discarded for various reasons.

Goals

Reflecting the diversity of the mission statement - education, research, and service - the goals of the Alumni Library consist of the following:

1. To select and acquire as much of the recorded knowledge of mankind as is consistent with the current and anticipated instructional and research needs of the university.

2. To process and organize the materials using modern technology applied through sound Library Science practice and to make the materials accessible in an attractive, intellectually stimulating atmosphere.

3. To instruct students in using the resources of the Alumni Library; and for the professional librarians to be viable members of the total educational operation on the Creighton University campus through individual and classroom instruction in bibliographic research and library use procedures.

4. To cooperate with other organizations for the advancement of scholarship, the effective use of resources, and the professional growth of the Alumni Library staff.

Elon College

THE ELON COLLEGE LIBRARY
MISSION STATEMENT

The primary objective of the Elon College Library is to provide materials and services which effectively implement, support, and enrich the educational program of the college.

To this end, The Board of Trustees of Elon College reaffirms the aims of the Charter of Elon College and asserts that the Library is to provide materials and services that will assist each student in his quest to acquire:

I. A philosophy of life which is founded upon and motivated by the beliefs and spiritual values of the historic Christian Church, and which will be reflected throughout his life in terms of high ethical standards, wholesome attitudes, and significant religious insights and devotion.

II. An understanding of his responsibilities and rights as a citizen in a democratic culture, a recognition of the intrinsic worth of other individuals, and intelligent awareness of world cultures, conditions, events, and issues.

III. A love of learning sufficient to promote his continued intellectual and cultural growth which comes out of sharing in an invigorating intellectual climate during his college career.

IV. A basic knowledge of the humanities, natural sciences, and social sciences, and an appreciation of the mutual relationships existing among these areas.

V. An understanding of the content and an achievement of competence in the procedures of at least one field of knowledge as preparation sufficient for graduate or professional study.

VI. The ability to think critically, logically, and creatively, and to communicate effectively by means of the written and spoken language.

VII. A sensibility to esthetic values through experience and study in the fine arts and opportunity to develop competence and excellence in the performing arts.

VIII. A knowledge of the principles of health and physical fitness, and skills useful for participation in wholesome recreational activities.

IX. A recognition of his abilities and aptitudes through counseling and guidance in the choice of an appropriate vocation.

P.O. Box 329, Evansville, Indiana 47702
(812) 479-2376

Clifford Memorial Library

Clifford Library and Learning Resources Mission

The Library and Learning Resources' mission reflects the mission of the University as a whole. That mission includes providing high quality value-oriented educational programs in the liberal arts and sciences and in selected professions. The University also stresses world-mindedness and serves the nontraditional as well as the traditional student by providing distinctive educational opportunities and experiences which reach beyond the campus.

The University of Evansville considers the library and its learning resources to be an integral element of the educational process. Recognizing that learning resources consist of a broad and expanding array of traditional and contemporary tools ranging from the basic monograph to the complex optical disc, the library and learning resources and services at the University of Evansville are organized under a single unit consisting of Clifford Memorial Library, the Music Library, the Center for Instructional Services, the University Archives, and the University Press. Such a structure enables the institution to provide the most comprehensive, efficient integrated resources and services.

Within this context the library unit seeks to achieve the following objectives:

1. To make available to the University community a collection of books, periodicals, and non-print materials which is as extensive and relevant to curricular offerings and research needs as possible;

2. To instruct and assist patrons in locating and using materials;

3. To manage these resources and services efficiently and effectively so as to provide the greatest benefit to the University.

Philosophy and Goals of

Loyola University Library

The Loyola University Library, in common with other academic libraries, is philosophically committed to providing resources appropriate to fostering academic excellence and freedom of inquiry. The library furthermore is committed to reflecting the uniquely Catholic and Jesuit character of the University, with its emphasis on undergraduate education, ethical development, and a Christian world-view.

The primary goal of the library is to provide those resources required to satisfy the undergraduate students' needs, be they for assigned, independent, or recommended use, or for personal enrichment and recreation, throughout their careers as undergraduates. The object is to provide a selection of materials to support the curriculum as well as a good, general, well-balanced collection. This collection should encompass the whole range of undergraduate studies and should be easily accessible and in an environment which is conducive to reading and learning and which also invites curiosity.

A secondary goal of the library is to provide resources required by graduate and undergraduate students and faculty for their scholarly research, but these materials are included in the undergraduate collection. Research materials not owned by the Loyola Library can be obtained for faculty and graduate students and selected undergraduate students on interlibrary loan, through membership in resource-sharing consortia such as the New Orleans Consortium and the Council on Academic Library Liaison, and through fee-for-service computerized bibliographic databases.

In addition, the Library recognizes its responsibility to reflect the unique status of the University community by collecting and retaining important material dealing with the Roman Catholic Church and the Society of Jesus.

Recognizing the unique historical and geographic characteristics of the community and region in which the University is located, the Library accepts responsibility for collecting, within constraints of space and budgets, materials dealing with the city of New Orleans, the state of Louisiana, and the lower Mississippi valley.

In keeping with these goals, it is the responsibility of the library to:

       1. Acquire and maintain intellectually balanced
          collections adequate to curriculum support,
          personal enrichment, citizen education, and

scholarly research needs. Policies of selection, retention, and disposal should reflect the current state of knowledge in relevant disciplines and should reflect all points of view.

2. Organize, house, circulate and publicize library materials effectively and efficiently in order to provide maximum accessibility to the collection.

3. Provide expert consultation and assistance to library users in locating information and materials, searching out and acquiring outside resources, and planning search strategies and initiating research projects.

4. Provide access to all current forms of information, including print, audio-visual, and computerized resources, together with appropriate organization, equipment and delivery methods to ensure that all formats are known and reasonably available to students and faculty.

The responsibility to select the appropriate materials to fulfill these needs rests jointly with the University Library Committee, the Library staff, and with every member of the University Faculty.

As one of the several major libraries in New Orleans, the Loyola Library can make efficient use of resources that may result from cooperation with other libraries. The Loyola library, therefore, should be committed to pursue the opportunities afforded by modern technologies and cooperative organization.

Approved, Library Faculty 11/16/79
Approved, University Library Committee, 11/28/79

Manhattanville College

MISSION OF THE LIBRARY

The fundamental purpose of the Manhattanville Library is to acquire, organize, and disseminate recorded information which supports the educational program of the College and which prepares the student to function responsibly as an individual within society. To this end the Library strives toward the following goals:

GOAL 1

To provide bibliographic, technological, and human resources which support curriculum and study by:

- Ensuring availability of facilities which enhance the educational process.

- Ensuring that the library faculty participates in the curriculum revision process.

- Furnishing library materials which support classroom instruction.

- Providing professional and support staff adequate to meet student demand for information.

- Adopting, for curriculum purposes, appropriate technology for information retrieval.

- Acquiring and organizing recorded information, regardless of physical format.

- Participating in the academic advising process.

GOAL 2

To teach students the skills needed to access recorded information by:

- Providing formal bibliographic instruction for preceptorial and advanced classes.

- Offering classes for students with special needs.

- Providing supplementary instruction to students who do not initially master required bibliographic skills.

- Reinforcing the instructional role of reference services.

- Offering individual tutorial sessions for independent student research.

University of Portland

LIBRARY

OBJECTIVES OF THE LIBRARY

The following statement of the objectives of the Wilson W. Clark Library
has been drawn up by the director and has been reviewed and accepted by
the professional staff and by the University Committee on the Library. It
has not been approved or reviewed by any other agency.

The Wilson W. Clark Memorial Library must serve the needs of a very
diversified clientele—from foreign students with minimal preparation
in the English language to faculty members doing doctoral and post-
doctoral research. The greatest concentration, however, is among the
undergraduates, and, therefore, the greatest expenditure of effort
and resources is devoted to fulfilling their needs.

The library must provide the materials necessary for study and
research. It must make these materials accessible to patrons by
providing assistance and instruction, from a qualified and adequate
staff, for those who are unfamiliar with library materials and
services. It must provide the environment and the facilities for
the effective use of scholarly materials.

The Collection

Since the primary purpose of the library is to serve the faculty and
students of the University in the pursuit of knowledge, materials will
be obtained and organized for use primarily so that the classroom
instruction of the faculty can be complemented and supplemented by
the library's collection. The library is also sensitive to the research
needs of members of the faculty. Material needed for such research
will be purchased if it is considered to be of general interest and
the budget will permit; otherwise every effort will be made to
obtain it on interlibrary loan. Selection of periodicals will generally
be guided by requests from the faculty, with emphasis on titles cited
in the standard periodical indexes.

Because a considerable number of students live on campus and do not
have ready access to the facilities of a public library, the University
library also has a responsibility to provide cultural and recreational
reading apart from the needs of the academic program. To this end,
at least some funds from the general budget will be used each year
for recreational type material. Subscriptions to a selection of
domestic and foreign newspapers will be maintained not only for use
as information sources, but also for their cultural and entertainment
value.

We have accepted at least some responsibility for being a repository for materials pertaining to the Catholic Church, particularly in the Pacific Northwest. Except for Mount Angel Abbey, we are the only Oregon college with the background and resources to provide the area with such materials. Therefore, in so far as our sources permit, we will attempt to purchase as widely as possible in the field of Catholic theology and literature.

In today's world, no librarian can hope to be sufficient unto itself. We need to share our resources with one another so that the academic needs of all may be fulfilled. We have a deep commitment to interlibrary cooperation and participate actively in a number of cooperative activities. Once our primary responsibility to the students and faculty of the University has been fulfilled, we feel that we have an obligation to share our resources with those who need them for scholarly work. And we in turn expect others to share with us.

Library Instruction

A library with the size and scope required to meet the needs of a university community is not easy to use. The identification and location of materials can be confusing until the user is shown how the system works.

Teaching students how to use the library is, therefore, a basic service which must be provided by the library staff. Since there is no regular academic course providing students with bibliographic instruction, the library staff will make known to the faculty their readiness to speak to individual classes about the library and its resources. The staff will also remember that individual reference encounters are an important opportunity for personalized instruction in methods of identifying and retrieving library materials. Work with patrons must have a double focus: that of discovering and delivering the materials which are needed and that of developing in patrons the confidence to ask for assistance when they need it.

The Staff

The professional library staff will be of sufficient size and competence to meet the legitimate needs of patrons. A master's degree in librarianship is a requirement for a professional position, and, while not absolutely necessary for entrance-level employment, a second master's degree will be required for promotion and tenure. In filling vacant positions, a diversity of educational backgrounds and subject specialities should be taken into consideration. Staff members should have other abilities besides bibliographic and library skills. The ability to teach on a one-to-one basis is important for all who interact with students. If orientation lectures and bibliographic instruction are to be successful, staff members must possess at least some skills in classroom teaching. They must be able to interact effectively with faculty in promoting use of library resources in conjunction with classroom activities. Above all, the staff must have sympathy for patrons and a concern for their needs so that they are made to feel comfortable in the library and are encouraged to ask for assistance.

The non-professional and student staff will be of sufficient size to assure the smooth functioning of all departments.

The Facilities

The environment of the library should encourage the use of the building and its resources. Hours of opening will be arranged to accomodate as many students as possible within constraints of staff and budget, and adjustments will be made to the schedule to provide extended hours before examinations.

Every effort will be made to maintain an atmosphere of quiet informality which will be conducive to effective study and research.

Pratt Institute

THE LIBRARY OF PRATT INSTITUTE

The Library of Pratt Institute has developed since 1887 and now serves the educational needs of approximately 4,300 undergraduate and graduate students in the Schools of Art and Design, Architecture, Engineering, Library and Information Science, and Liberal Arts and Science. The Library's collections are vital to the continued excellence of the Institute's academic programs and to its ability to attract and retain the quality of faculty and students it desires. The collection encompasses works of a variety of disciplines taught at Pratt and is particularly noteworthy in the fields of art and architecture. Through participation in cooperative programs and interlibrary loans, the Library is also an important element in a resource-sharing system among the Academic Libraries of Brooklyn.

Objectives of the Pratt Library

Purpose

The purpose of the Pratt Library is to provide recorded information in all of the subject fields pertinent to the Institute's educational goals and needed by students, the academic and the administrative staff of Pratt Institute.

Role

The Library strives to fulfill this purpose by:

1. Identifying and acquiring (or otherwise making available) library materials in all formats needed for instruction and research within the Institute.

2. Developing reference, bibliographic, and other specialized library services that effectively and imaginatively reinforce academic objectives.

3. Making resources accessible through the support services and facilities of specialized library units.

4. Assuring the security and integrity of the collections.

Program Objectives

These general statements suggest the range of specific objectives guiding the Pratt Institute Library as it seeks to achieve its purpose and fulfill its role. The Library will:

72

1. Assist users in the understanding of the organization of library resources, identifying and locating recorded information, and utilizing library services.

2. Have needed materials readily available to Pratt students and academic staff, and others, as appropriate, whether from Pratt collections or on loan from other libraries.

3. Select and acquire the information resources most needed to support the instructional and research programs of Pratt.

4. House library collections and service activities in space that meets staff and user requirements, assure collection security, safeguard the condition of resources, and enhance operating performance of the Library's staff.

5. Maintain and, when possible, improve the physical condition of materials in the collections, with special attention to protecting unique items and distinctive categories of materials.

6. Develop better ways to offer library resources and to provide additional services for users as means for improving the quality of academic programs and the effectiveness of instructional activity.

7. Maintain purposeful working relationships with academic departments and with other offices of the Institute to help assure development of library capabilities that are consistent with academic objectives and Institute plans.

8. Create opportunities for individual staff members to define and achieve their career goals in the context of the general objectives and staffing requirements of the Library.

9. Promote and create constructive working relationships with other academic libraries and related organizations to obtain access to resources and to effect development of programs of many kinds that would meet needs of users and improve performance of individual libraries.

10. Enhance knowledge of library procedures and facilitate decision making by the maintenance of accurate statistical and other departmental records.

WOLFGRAM MEMORIAL LIBRARY

Widener University

MISSION

The Wolfgram Memorial Library functions as the major resource for recorded knowledge and information in support of the University's instructional, research, cultural,
and administrative programs. This responsibility is twofold:

a. To collect and organize appropriate library materials;

b. To establish and maintain services for optimal access and use of the library's
    resources and of other available and useful information networks.

GOALS

In order to fulfill the responsibilities implied in the mission statement, the
library must have the following:

1. A collection of library materials maintained and developed at a level appro-
    priate to support ongoing university programs

2. Services to assist the primary users, i.e. the university community, for
    optimal access and utilization of library resources

3. Programs to teach skills of information retrieval and use, necessary in
    our information society

4. Organization and procedures for the library's collections and services according
    to the most advanced, efficient methods

5. Participation in support and development of networks and other resource sharing
    arrangements, for reciprocal exchange of library materials and access to out-
    side information sources needed for teaching, learning, and research

6. Professional and support staff with motivation, training, skills, and compatible
    personal goals providing the essential element necessary to maintain the highest
    standards in library services

7. Adequate budget and other financial and administrative support to establish and
    maintain appropriate standards for university-level library services

Fall 1983

Public Institutions (Under 2500 Students)

The facilities and staff of the Williams Library at Northern State College support the college's mission in instruction, public service, and research. In order to carry out its assigned mission, the library provides library services, audiovisual services and television services. In 1980 the Williams Library adopted the following goals.

1.0   GOALS

1.1   To provide information sources and services appropriate to user needs, to devise delivery systems, and to facilitate maximum access to information.

  A. Identifying the information needs of users.
  B. Helping users to identify, evaluate, and select materials which are appropriate to their needs, interests, and teaching/learning styles.
  C. Organizing and indexing information.
  D. Providing reference service to users.
  E. Providing bibliographic service to users.
  F. Promoting functional knowledge of a variety of resources and of approaches to obtaining information.
  G. Providing access to information available from outside agencies, including networks.
  H. Stimulating effective utilization of library and media personnel and resources for the improvement of instruction and for curriculum development.

1.2   To provide consultation services.

  A. Supporting curriculum development and implementation with respect to necessary print and non-print materials.
  B. Recommending print and non-print applications to accomplish specific instructional purposes.
  C. Serving as instructional resource consultants and materials specialists to the divisions of the college.
  D. Developing user understanding of the strengths and limitations of various information delivery systems.
  E. Assisting in planning and modifying physical facilities to provide effective learning environments.

1.3   To provide design services within established college priorities.

    A. Planning and evaluating library/audiovisual services programs.
    B. Supporting instructional improvement and implementation.
    C. Developing materials for self-instructional use by learners for specialized objectives.
    D. Helping determine the effectiveness and validity of instructional materials for learning sequences.
    E. Providing materials and production services for the support of instructional.

1.4   To provide administrative services which support program goals and priorities.

    A. Formulating library and media program purposes.
    B. Establishing library and media services policies.
    C. Identifying library and media services program priorities.
    D. Establishing criteria for decision making in library and media services areas, such as the selection of personnel, selection and circulation of materials and equipment, and technical processing.
    E. Developing the library and media budget in consultation with faculty and administration.
    F. Supervising library and media services personnel.
    G. Developing functional specifications for new library and media equipment.
    H. Establishing and maintaining library and media services access and delivery systems.
    I. Establishing and maintaining library and media production services.
    J. Providing for maintenance of library and media services, materials equipment, and facilities.
    K. Implementing a library and media services public information program.
    L. Providing appropriate environment and space for the utilization of information sources and services.

2.0   GOVERNANCE

2.1   Authority

The professional staff of library and media services is charged with the responsibility and accompanying authority to establish and supervise the procedures of their respective departments based on established written policy and written job descriptions. All policies shall be consistent with the collective bargaining contract currently in force.

2.2   The Library professional staff meets on a regularly scheduled basis to consider the needs of their areas including, but not confined to, policy, procedure, personnel, schedule, budget. The mode of decision making is normally by consensus. Minutes of these meetings shall be kept. The secretary shall forward a copy of the minutes of each meeting to the Dean for his/her information.

2.3   One member shall be appointed annually, on a rotating basis, to serve
       as secretary.   The secretary shall be responsible for recording,
       distributing, and maintaining a file of minutes for all regularly called
       faculty meetings. The secretary shall also be responsible for receiving
       and publishing agenda items prior to each meeting.

2.4   The professional staff may meet independent of the Director to
       consider matters or conditions of employment and collective
       bargaining recommendations and agreements.

Public Institutions (2500 Students And Over)

Austin Peay State University

Felix G. Woodward Library Mission Statement

The mission of the Library is to provide materials and services which support the University's instruction, research, and public service mission. The goals of the Library in the pursuit of its mission are to provide the library materials, services, and facilities necessary to support the University's instructional programs, to foster faculty research and scholarship, to meet student course-and non-course-related library needs, and to augment library resources available to the non-University community. The Library pursues these goals through the objectives of acquiring, organizing, and maintaining the requisite equipment and materials in their various formats, providing production of audiovisual media, and by creating a physical environment conducive to user needs and media requirements. The stated goals and objectives of the Library are:

I. To provide the quantity and types of library materials necessary to support the University's instructional and research mission.

    A. To insure that the materials the Library acquires meet in priority order the purpose of: (1) supporting student and faculty scholarship relative to the curricula; (2) contributing to the maintenance of a current general reference collection; (3) representing world culture; (4) providing recreational reading for students; and (5) serving as a seedbed for faculty research.

    B. To provide additional resources and means of access to resources through interlibrary loan and computerized information retrieval.

II. To make materials accessible by controlling them bibliographically, organizing them into collections, and maintaining means of access to them.

    A. To establish bibliographic control over books and audiovisual media by following accepted standards and practice of descriptive cataloging and for the choice and form of entry.

    B. To maintain for books and audiovisual media a means of access which provides a record of each unique item in the Library by author and/or title and groups such items by common subject according to accepted standards and practice.

C. To organize book and audiovisual media into collections by classifying them according to Library of Congress Classification System and by following Library of Congress practice for call number construction.

D. To maintain a means of access to periodicals that makes them readily retrievable in their various formats.

E. To organize federal government publications into a separate collection according to the Superintendent of Documents Classification System and to maintain holdings and receipt records according to Government Printing Office regulations.

III. To make the Library collections and other Library resources available to Library patrons.

A. To provide formal bibliographic and general library instruction.

B. To increase and maintain the efficiency of the interlibrary loan service and to operate the service in accordance with the National Interlibrary Loan Code, the Tennessee Interlibrary Loan Code, the Copyright Act of 1978, and the CONTU Guidelines.

C. To provide an effective means for the circulation of Library materials and to insure their return.

D. To keep materials on shelves in correct call number order for easy access.

E. To house course related reserve materials for students.

F. To produce audiovisual software and provide individualized and group instruction in media production techniques.

G. To locate bibliographic citations and other information obtained most efficiently from national databases in response to requests by University faculty, students, and staff.

H. To generate awareness of and interest in online searching among members of the Library and University communities.

IV. To have the facilities and technology necessary for the effective utilization of Library resources.

A. To plan and execute the physical arrangement of Library services and access.

B. To acquire new equipment for Library operations as needed.

C. To maintain copy machines for public use and for producing paper copies from microforms.

D. To maintain exit security to protect Library materials.

E. To provide audiovisual equipment and maintenance of University audiovisual equipment.

V. To maintain an organizational structure and operation conducive to the effective pursuit of the Library's mission.

A. To maintain and develop an effective Library staff.

B. To guarantee fiscal responsibility in expending appropriated Library funds.

C. To monitor and adjust departmental staffing patterns as needed.

D. To foster effective internal Library communication.

E. To maintain communications between the Library and the University community.

VI. To participate in and contribute to local, state, regional, and national cooperative library activities.

A. To enter Library holdings into the OCLC database.

B. To retain membership in the Southeastern Library Network (SOLINET) and the State Board of Regents Media Consortium.

C. To fill interlibrary loan requests from other libraries expeditiously.

D. To participate in other types of resource sharing as is feasible.

November 1, 1982

MISSION OF THE DANIEL LIBRARY

The mission of the Daniel Library is to provide those basic resources necessary to support the Citadel's academic programs and purposes. To achieve this, it must be recognized that a library is more than a collection of books; it is a collection of informational materials, arranged in an orderly manner and manned by competent personnel to make that material readily and easily available. In order to fully appreciate the needs and demands for library , a library committee representing a cross section of the faculty and student body has been appointed. This committee formulates policy and the Library Director and his staff administer that policy in keeping with college regulations.

Midwestern State University

The university library is the most important intellectual resource of the academic community. As such, its primary mission is to provide materials and services that complement the curricula and support the objectives of the parent institution. The academic library also serves as a capability which affords sutdents an opportunity for independent study outside the course offerings of the institution. In addition, the academic library must strive to meet the changing needs of all its patrons-- from the beginning freshman to the senior research professor. Furthermore, the library, especially that of a public institution, has an obligation to the community of which it is a part. The library should serve as an information center for that community so long as such service does not conflict with the needs of the university. The library also serves a teaching function, both for students and faculty, as well as providing support for the research and public service programs of the parent institution.

In an attempt to fulfill this mission, Moffett Library has compiled a list of goals and objectives. The objectives address the staff, the collections, the services, and automation.

THE STAFF

1. More regularly scheduled staff meetings, at least once a quarter.

    a. To provide more avenues of communication among the departments.

    b. To provide input/feedback to the Director.

2. More in-service training at all levels.

   a. To update skills in all areas.

   b. To serve as a current awareness vehicle.

3. Hire a Collection Development Librarian.
   (This has been accomplished)

4. Hire an audio-visual technican/assistant.

THE COLLECTION

1. Periodic survey/analysis of user needs.

2. Continue to concentrate on the addition of quality materials with the help of a Collection Development Librarian.

3. Strive to maintain a well-balanced collection that supports the university's curricula.

4. To adhere to the philosophy expressed in the Library's collection development policy.

5. Secure at least one copy of every university publication for the library.

6. Develop, promote the Rare Book Collection.

LIBRARY SERVICES

1. Continue the program of educating the library user--through tours, classroom presentations, and on a one-to-one basis.

2. Work toward including the library in the orientation process, both for students and faculty.

3. Closer contact/cooperation with the teaching faculty.

PHYSICAL FACILITIES

1. Strive to improve the physical facilities, either through support for a new building or an addition to the present one.

2. Make the best possible use of the space available.

3. Install book detection system.

PUBLIC RELATIONS

1. Continue to promote resource sharing/library cooperation possibly through an area library association.

2. Establish a "Friends of the Library" group.

3. Publish periodic newsletter.

4. Feasibility study for library handbook.

AUTOMATION

1. Work with computing cneter to acquire new circulation system.

2. Cooperate fully with the center and with other users to enhance computing capabilities.

3. Continue to plan/develop an automated acquisitions system.

4. Continue to monitor OCLC'c Serials system to determine feasibility for use.

5. Plan for eventual on-line card catalog.

6. Plan for on-line access to serials holdings.

University of Wisconsin-Parkside

The University of Wisconsin-Parkside, one of thirteen degree-granting campuses in the University of Wisconsin system, was authorized by the State Legislature in 1965.

The 700 acre campus, located in southeastern Wisconsin's urban industrial corridor between Milwaukee and Chicago, opened in 1969. Situated on the outskirts of Racine and Kenosha, UW-Parkside offers a full range of liberal arts majors as well as professional and pre-professional studies in such areas as business, engineering, education, allied health, and computer and applied sciences. The academic programs were designed to focus on the many interrelated social, economic, educational, environmental, political and cultural concerns with accompany life in an urban-industrial society. This educational focus, called the "Industrial Society Mission," is designed to provide students with a grasp of human and technological resources demanded by the highly urbanized and industrial character of the region.

The Library/Learning Center's role within the University is to participate actively in its instructional process as a "teaching library." Teaching library refers to a library which is not only a support service for academic programs but which itself is actively and directly involved in implementing UW-Parkside's efforts in the areas of teaching, research and community service.

Library/Learning Center
Mission and Goals

The mission of the Library/Learning Center is to assume an active role in the development of the community's* human resources by implementing fully the concept of a teaching library. The Library/Learning Center aims to fulfill this mission by:

(a) developing an organized collection of materials and equipment and providing access to other resources which best satsify the present and future needs of the University relating to its teaching, research, and community service responsibilities;

(b) encouraging and facilitating life-long learning through the development of instructional programs and services which emphasize investigative and information managment skills;

(c) providing distinctive programs and services designed to meet the intellectual and cultural needs of an information-based society.

Library Learning Center Goals

To carry out its mission the Library/Learning Center has set the following goals:

1. To plan, develop, and implement L/LC policies and programs that are compatible with the University's mission and interpret them to the community.

2. To support the current and future curriculum, research and other information needs of the University by selecting, acquiring, organizing, preserving, and circulating a collection of materials in a variety of formats (e.g., print and audio visual materials, computer software and databases) as well as equipment necessary for its use.

3. To provide comprehensive L/LC orientation and instruction enabling all users to locate, evaluate, manage and present information.

4. To interpret the collection to all users, assist them in the utilization of the L/LC's as well as other electronically available databases, provide referral to additional information sources and supply individualized assistance in using instructional materials.

5. To enrich the University curriculum by cooperating with faculty and staff in the design, development, and production of instructional programs and materials.

6. To assist in the development of a local and inter institutional academic information management networks.

7. To evaluate the collection, programs, and facilities in order to improve the effectiveness and efficiency of services.

8. To promote cultural and intellectual activity by offering programs, facilities, and services to the community.

9. To share resources, services, and ideas by cooperating with all areas of the University as well as professional, public, and private organizations and institutions in the community.

10. To encourage personal and professional growth by providing staff development opportunities for all L/LC employees.

* The term "community" whenever it is used in this document refers to the faculty, staff, and students of the University of Wisconsin-Parkside as well as the people, agencies, institutions and businesses of the surrounding area.

Regional Accreditation Agencies' Statements

.

MIDDLE STATES ASSOCIATION OF COLLEGES AND SCHOOLS

LIBRARY/LEARNING RESOURCES

Nature

The library/learning resources center is of paramount importance to the students and faculty. The types and variety of books and other materials will depend on the nature of the institution and they must relate realistically to the institution's educational goals, curricula, size, complexity or degree level, and the diversity of its teaching, learning, and research requirements. The centrality of a library/learning resources center in the educational mission of an institution deserves more than rhetoric and must be supported by more than lip service.

Holdings and Utilization

The extent of a library/learning resources center's holdings must be in reasonable proportion to the needs to be served, but numbers alone are no assurance of excellence. The quality of the holdings, their current relevance to the institution's educational programs, and the frequency of their use are important characteristics of an effective library/learning resources center. Faculty must lead the way in demonstrating the importance of books and other materials in their teaching and research while simultaneously encouraging their students in those intellectual endeavors which enliven learning and induce habitual use of books and other learning resources. The faculty and library staff need to work closely together in planning the development and employment of the library/learning resources center to achieve their educational objectives.

Scope

A library/learning resources center needs to reveal the general scope of the learned and creative world, fostering broad interests among its users by surrounding them with basic interpretive books and periodicals, journals, non-print materials, and standard reference works in the general fields of learning. They must encourage cultural breadth and intellectual depth as well as practical competence, and there should be some provision for recreational reading matter. The increasing availability of cultural and specialized information on tape, records, and film should be drawn upon in developing the strength and quality of the library/learning resources center, and cooperative arrangements with networks and neighboring libraries are encouraged as means of greatly enhancing an institution's resources.

Staffing

The librarians and other professional staff must demonstrate their competence using criteria comparable to those of other faculty and staff, and be given sufficient responsibility and funds to facilitate optimum functioning. Status and privileges of library/learning resources center staff should be commensurate with the significance and responsibilities of their positions. The library/learning resources center in the best sense is a classroom, and the level of excellence in the professional staff is measurable in part to the extent that they are active participants in teaching and learning, not merely custodians of books, reference collections, or other institutional materials and equipment.

Environmental Factors

A fine building does make a good library/learning resources center, but an excellent collection is useless unless it is available. Seating, lighting, arrangement of books, acoustical treatment and the like are to be judged by their serviceability in making the library/learning resources center an attractive place for study. Nothing else matters much if the facilities are not used.

Reprinted with permission from Commission on Higher Education, Characteristics of Excellence: Standards for Accreditation (Philadelphia, Pennsylvania: Middle States Association of Colleges and Schools, 1982), pp. 23-25.

NEW ENGLAND ASSOCIATION OF SCHOOLS AND COLLEGES, INC.

THE SANBORN HOUSE, 15 HIGH STREET, WINCHESTER, MASSACHUSETTS 01890
(617) 729-6762

COMMISSION ON INSTITUTIONS OF HIGHER EDUCATION

March 23, 1984

Mr. Larry Hardesty
Director of Library Services
Eckerd College
St. Petersburg, FL   33733

Dear Mr. Hardesty:

I am responding to your letter requesting information on
this association's policy on library objectives.

The Commission's standard on Library and Learning Resources,
a copy of which is enclosed, does not call for an explicit
statement of library objectives. However, institutional
resources, including the library, are expected to support
the institution's mission and objectives; each library is
therefore evaluated in respect to the particular institution's nature, size, programs, degree levels, and the like.
The Commission does not enforce the standards of other professional associations, such as the ALA or ACRL, although
the librarian on a visiting team is likely to be familiar
with ALA standards and to use them as a general frame of
reference.

In the next couple of years, the Commission's Standards for
Accreditation will be revised, and the standard on Library
will undoubtedly be expanded. Whether there will be a
specific reference to library objectives, I cannot say.

I hope that this information is helpful to you.

Sincerely,

Millicent Kalaf

MK:fb
Enclosure

1885 1985

NEW ENGLAND ASSOCIATION OF SCHOOLS & COLLEGES, INC.

COMMISSION ON INSTITUTIONS OF HIGHER EDUCATION

March 21, 1985

Dr. Larry Hardesty
Director of Library Services
Eckerd College
St. Petersburg, FL 33733

Dear Dr. Hardesty:

I am responding to your recent request for additional
information about this Commission's standards for college libraries.

There have been no changes in our standards or guidelines for libraries since your inquiry a year ago. The
Commission does not request mission statements from
libraries, although any such statements should be consistent with the overall mission of the institution and
with its programs and degree levels. The absence of a
library statement of objectives would not necessarily
be considered a "deficiency", but an institutional self-
study is expected to address "the philosophy utilized in
providing library/learning resource services."

I hope that this information is helpful to you.

Sincerely,

Millicent Kalaf

MK/mmw

Standards for Accreditation

LIBRARY AND LEARNING RESOURCES

The institution should provide those learning resources necessary to support "the educational program" and the intellectual and cultural development of faculty and students.

The institution should have its own library or collection of learning resources. Collections of print and non-print materials should be appropriate to the range and complexity of the educational program, to each curriculum of studies, and to student enrollment. Materials should be housed in convenient locations and readily accessible to students.

Adequate study space should be provided. The collection should be administered by a professionally qualified and numerically adequate staff.

The exchange of materials and services with other academic or local libraries and within library networks is encouraged.

Reprinted with permission from Commission on Institutions of Higher Education, Standards for Accreditation (Winchester, Massachusetts: New England Association of Schools and Colleges, Inc., March 1984), p. 8.

NCA

North Central Association
of Colleges and Schools
**Commission on Institutions
of Higher Education**

159 North Dearborn
Chicago, Illinois 60601
(312) 263-0456
(800) 621-7440

February 19, 1985

Dr. Larry Hardesty
Director of Library Services
Eckerd College
St. Petersburg, Florida 33733

Dear Dr. Hardesty:

Thank you for your letter of last month which the Director of the Commission has
forwarded to me for reply. When visiting teams evaluate an institution, libraries and
library resources are certainly a matter of major concern. We do not, however,
require that an institution have a library statement of objectives. If one does exist,
I think it is likely that a team will examine it and judge the library, at least in part,
in relation to it. We do not have any specific guidelines for developing such a
statement, and so long as the visiting team and those involved in the review process
are satisfied that an institution's library resources are sufficient in light of the
overall purposes of the institution, it is unlikely that the presence or lack of such a
statement would be an issue. Our consultant-evaluator corps consists of more than
700 faculty and administrators from our member institutions so it is reasonable to
expect that there would be differing opinions on how best to assure and promote
library development.

I am sorry that I cannot give more specific answers to your questions, but hope that
this explanation is helpful to you. Thank you for your interest in te North Central
Association and its activities.

Yours sincerely,

Jean Mather

Jean Mather
Assistant Director

NORTHWEST ASSOCIATION OF SCHOOLS AND COLLEGES

COMMISSION ON COLLEGES
Office of the Executive Director

March 22, 1984

Mr. Larry Hardesty
Director of Library Services
Eckerd College
St. Petersburg, Florida 33733

Dear Mr. Hardesty:

In reply to your letter of March 1, we are enclosing a copy of our
Accreditation Standards. Under Standard VI, Library and Learning
Resources it is noted that the goals and objectives of the library must
be compatible with and supportive of the institutional goals and objectives.
In the self-study each institution is required to provide a written
statement of the philosophy, goals and objectives of the library and
learning resources program and to make an analysis of the program in
relation to the overall philosophy and goals of the institution. The
statement and analysis of the goals and objectives of the library are
evaluated as part of the on-site evaluation by a team of peers. If the
institution did not have a statement of goals and objectives for the
library, and the goals and objectives were not analyzed in relation to the
goals and objectives of the institution, the institution would be considered
deficient in this area.

Sincerely yours,

James F. Bemis
Executive Director

JFB:b
Enclosure

3700-B University Way N.E., Seattle, Washington 98105 Telephone (206) 543-0195

NORTHWEST ASSOCIATION OF SCHOOLS AND COLLEGES

COMMISSION ON COLLEGES
Office of the Executive Director

February 4, 1985

Dr. Larry Hardesty
Director of Library Services
Eckerd College
St. Petersburg, Florida 33733

Dear Dr. Hardesty:

In reply to your letter of January 25, our standard on the Library and
Learning Resources require that the Library have goals and objectives that
are compatible with and supportive of the institutional goals and objectives.
In the Library and Learning Resources section of the institutional self-
study we ask for, among other things:

> . a written statement of the philosophy, goals and
> objectives of the library and learning resources
> program;
>
> . a list of all services which support the institution's
> goals and objectives.

Beyond the description, the institution is also asked to analyze and appraise
its goals, objectives and services. We do not provide guidelines for the
development of a statement on library goals and objectives.

The on-site evaluation committee is provided instructions which include
the library and learning resources. Every report of an evaluation committee
covers the library and learning resources. If an institution being evaluated
does not have a written statement of its philosophy, goals and objectives
for the library and learning resources program, it would be considered a
deficiency and should be noted in the report of the evaluation committee.

The institutional self-studies and evaluation committee reports are not
available for distribution through this office. Should you want to receive
sample documents, it would be necessary to request them from the institutions.

Best wishes for the successful completion of your survey.

Sincerely yours,

James F. Bemis
Executive Director

JFB:b

3700-B University Way N.E., Seattle, Washington 98105   Telephone (206) 543-0195

IV. LIBRARY AND LEARNING RESOURCES

Standard

The purpose of a library and learning resources program is to support and improve instruction and learning in ways consistent with the philosophy and evolving curricular programs of the institution. Its goals and objectives. It shall constitute a central support of the entire educational program and assist in the cultural development of students, faculty, and the community it serves. It shall be capable of supporting basic research in academic majors, to the level of degrees offered. It shall provide services, resources, and facilities which encourage and stimulate such activities as individualization of instruction, independent study, innovation, effective use of resources, and community involvement.

Facilities, materials, and equipment shall be provided at a level of quality and quantity which will support and enhance the educational philosophy, goals, and objectives of the institution. Facilities shall be adequate to accomodate a satisfactory percentage of users in an inviting and efficient atmosphere. Materials shall have the depth and breadth appropriate for the achievement of the goals and objectives of the library and learning resources program. Equipment shall be available in sufficient variety and quantity to serve the needs of the users.

Services include providing convenient and comprehensive access to library and learning resources, assisting in effective utilization of the library and resources, providing instructional and faculty development functions, such as design and production of instructional materials, and use of the administrator(s) of the library and learning resources program.

The library and learning resources program shall be administered as part of the instructional program by qualified professional staff, with representatives of the faculty acting in an advisory capacity. The number of library and learning resources personnel and their competencies must be based upon the specific objectives established for the program.

Wherever an institution provides programs, it must demonstrate that library and learning resources services, fully adequate to the programs, are conveniently available and used by students and faculty.

Occasionally an institution will make library and learning resources services available to students and faculty through specific arrangements with another institution or other agencies where the holdings and services are adequate to support the programs and capable of maintaining an adequate level of support. In such cases, it is incumbent upon the institution to demonstrate that these arrangements are fully effective, will continue to be so in the forseeable future, and are capable of meeting the needs of prospective program changes and additions.

SOUTHERN ASSOCIATION OF COLLEGES AND SCHOOLS

795 Peachtree Street, N.E. • Atlanta, Georgia 30365
Phone 897-6100 Area Code 404

February 1, 1985

Dr. Larry Hardesty
Director of Library Services
Eckerd College
St. Petersburg, Florida 33733

Dear Dr. Hardesty:

This letter is in answer to yours of January 25, 1985, in which you ask what
use is made of library missions statements in the accreditation process.

As you are probably aware, the College Delegate Assembly adopted in December
1984 new Criteria to be used to accredit and to reaffirm accreditation of
institutions of higher learning. I am enclosing a xeroxed copy of the
section on library. You will note that there is a statement that each
institution must develop for its library a mission statement consistent with
the institutional purposes. Further it is required that the library be
evaluated on a regular basis. The visiting committee is supposed to check
to determine if the library does have a clearly stated mission which gives
the goals and purposes of the library. If not, the committee usually will
recommend that such a statement be developed.

Therefore, to answer your question, the mission statement is requested and
is reviewed during the accreditation process. We do not have any specific
guidelines as to the development of such mission statements, leaving it to
the individual institutions. However, we do have it as a deficiency if an
institution does not have a library missions statement.

Sincerely yours,

Henry L. Ashmore
Interim/Executive Director
Commission on Colleges

HLA/ml

100

Section V
Educational Support Services

5.1 EDUCATIONAL SUPPORT SERVICES

Each institution must provide a variety of services that support its educational purposes. These support services include the library; instructional support services; computer services; and those services that complement the educational, social, moral, and physical development of the student.

Each institution has the responsibility to establish staffing, programs, and services for educational support which will reflect:
- the nature of the student population;
- the primary educational goals of the institution;
- the opportunities for learning that must be present in the total educational program in order to achieve the primary educational goals;
- the programs and services necessary to achieve the educational goals of the institution;
- the human, physical and fiscal resources required for the effective implementation of these services and programs.

5.2 LIBRARY

Because the library is essential to learning, each institution must have a library which provides the primary and secondary materials needed to support its purpose and programs. These resources should be available in a well-equipped, readily accessible facility of adequate size which encourages maximum use by the campus community. To facilitate use of such resources, both on and off campus, a competent staff must be available to assist the users. The collections of print and non-print materials must be well organized, adequate hours must be maintained to ensure accessibility to users.

Priorities for acquiring materials and establishing services must be determined with the needs of the users in mind. Thus, with active cooperation of the administration, faculty, students and library staff, each institution must develop for its library a mission statement consistent with the institutional purpose. The library must be evaluated regularly and systematically to ensure that it is meeting the needs of its users and supporting the programs and purpose of the institution.

5.2.1 Services

Basic library services must include: an orientation program designed to teach new users how to obtain individual assistance; access to bibliographic information; and access to materials. Any one of a variety of methods, or a combination of them, may be used for this purpose: formal instruction, lectures, library guides and user aids, self-paced instruction and computer assisted instruction.

The library should offer point-of-use instruction, personal assistance in conducting library research and traditional reference services. Professional assistance should be available at convenient locations when the library is open.

The library must provide adequate records of on-campus materials through catalogs, indexes and bibliographies; access to information sources regardless of location through standard indexes and bibliographies; and, where appropriate, access to external bibliographic data bases.

The library must have adequate physical facilities to house, service and make the library collections easily available; up-to-date equipment in good condition for using print and non-print materials; provision for rapid access to any remotely stored materials; provision for interlibrary loan agreements; and an efficient and appropriate circulation system. The library must provide students with opportunities to learn how to access information in a variety of formats so that they can continue life-long learning. Librarians must work cooperatively with the teaching faculty in assisting students to use resources materials effectively.

An institution must provide appropriate library services at off-campus locations where credit courses are offered to ensure that these courses receive the same level of library support as that given to equivalent on-campus courses. This obligation can be met by developing a branch library or making contractual arrangements with libraries in the geographic area. Competent library personnel should be assigned the planning duties entailed in providing these services and in ascertaining their continued adequacy. When contractual agreements are reached, they must specify the level of service and type of access to be provided for students and faculty.

5.2.2 Collections

The library collections must be sufficient to support the educational, research and public service programs of the institution. Institutions offering graduate work must provide library resources substantially beyond those required for the bachelor's degree. Librarians, teaching faculty and researchers must share in the development of collections and the institution must establish policies defining their involvement.

Each library must have a policy governing the principles of selection and weeding.

5.2.3 Staff

The library must be adequately staffed by professional librarians who hold professional degrees at the graduate level in library science or learning resources. Since professional or technical training in specialized areas is increasingly important in meeting user needs, professionals with specialized non-library degrees may be employed, where appropriate, to supervise these areas.

The library support staff must be adequate to carry out responsibilities of a non-professional nature. Qualifications (skills needed) for these support positions be defined by the institution.

The chief librarian must be a well-qualified professional whose administration of library services contributes to the educational effectiveness of the institution. Organizational relationships, both external and internal to the library, should be clearly specified. Institutional policies concerning faculty status, salary and contractual security for library personnel must be clearly defined and made known to all personnel at the time of employment.

5.2.4 Institutional Relationships

In order to increase ability of the library to provide the resources and services needed by its users, cooperative relationships with other libraries and agencies should be considered. However, these cooperative relationships must not be used by institutions to avoid responsibility for providing their own adequate and accessible library resources and services. In all cases of cooperative arrangements, formal agreements must be established, thereby safeguarding the integrity and continuity of library resources and services. The effectiveness of such cooperative arrangements must be regularly evaluated.

Reprinted with permission from Commission on Colleges, "Criteria for Accreditation," (Atlanta, Georgia: Southern Association of Colleges and Schools, December 1984), pp. 21-23.

WESTERN ASSOCIATION OF SCHOOLS AND COLLEGES

Accrediting Commission for Senior Colleges and Universities

BOX 9990, MILLS COLLEGE, OAKLAND, CALIFORNIA 94613-0990

(415) 632-5000

OFFICERS

Chairman
DAVID L. COLE
　(Emeritus) Occidental College

Vice Chairman
PAUL A. ALBRECHT
　Claremont Graduate School/
　University Center

Executive Director
KAY J. ANDERSEN

Associate Executive Director
RALPH A. WOLFF

MEMBERS

E.J. ANDERSON
　Pacific Union Conference
　of Seventh-Day Adventists

JEWEL PLUMMER COBB
　California State University,
　Fullerton

JAMES F. DEITZ
　Heald Colleges

ELLEN H. ELLIS
　Public Member

ESTHER FULLER
　Public Member

GAIL FULLERTON
　San Jose State University

DONALD L. GARRITY
　Central Washington
　University

HAZEL J. JONES
　(Retired) California Polytechnic
　State University,
　San Luis Obispo

GRACE H. LARSEN
　Holy Names College

PAUL L. LOCATELLI, S.J.
　University of Santa Clara

ROBERT W. MAC VICAR
　Oregon State University

WILLIAM W. MAY
　University of Southern
　California

MARY METZ
　Mills College

JAMES H. MEYER
　University of California,
　Davis

MAYNARD TOLL
　Public Member

BEATRICE T. YAMASAKI
　University of Hawaii,
　Manoa

OFFICE STAFF

EVELYN M. THORNE
　Administrative Assistant

DELSIE M. AUSTINSON
　Secretary

January 31, 1985

Dr. Larry Hardesty
Director of Library Services
Eckerd College
St. Petersburg, FL 33733

Dear Dr. Hardesty:

We do not ask libraries to prepare a statement of
objectives, but I think it would be a good idea.
We will consider including it as part of the next
Handbook Revision. I have enclosed Standard Six
which deals with Library, Computer, and Other
Learning Resources.

Sincerely,

Kay J. Andersen
Executive Director

KJA:dma

Enclosure

WESTERN ASSOCIATION OF SCHOOLS AND COLLEGES

STANDARD SIX: LIBRARY,
COMPUTER, AND OTHER
LEARNING RESOURCES

Standard 6.A. Quality of Holdings

Library holdings, computers, and other learning resources are sufficient in quantity, depth, diversity, and currentness to support all the institution's academic offerings at appropriate levels.

All resources of a college or university exist to implement the educational program and thereby accomplish institutional purposes. Learning resources include facilities, equipment, materials, persons, and software which augment the curricular offerings. Examples are the library facility with its collections, equipment, and the more modern electronic design/production/distribution of curricular support information; tele-communications including radio and microwave; and computer support in the form of access to hardware, software, documentation, and support personnel.

Learning resources encompass instructional development functions as well as direct instructional service.

For most colleges and universities, learning resources are a central support to the educational program. Both collection requirements and the service program will differ depending on the purposes and programs of the institution. An institution offering graduate work, especially doctoral study, is expected to have major holdings, including serials, in all of its graduate areas.

Some, though by no means all, components of this standard are:

6.A.1 A wide variety of learning resources—both holdings and facilitating equipment—is available for alternate modes of instruction suited to a variety of student needs and learning styles.

6.A.2 Library holdings and equipment are sufficient in quantity and quality to meet the needs of the curriculum and the students. Inter-library loan arrangements are established and used.

6.A.3 Library holdings and equipment are balanced in direct relationship to the nature and level of curricular offerings.

6.A.4 Efforts are made to identify and replace lost books or holdings and damaged or outdated equipment, and a long-range plan has been developed which includes provision for meeting any deficiencies; provisions are made for the security and preservation of the collection.

6.A.5 Media equipment and materials and learning support systems are adequate, well-maintained, and readily accessible to faculty and students.

6.A.6 In major libraries automated on-line bibliographic data systems are incorporated as appropriate in support of technical and public service activities.

Standard 6.B. Acquisition Procedures

The selection and evaluation of library and resource materials are cooperative endeavors requiring strong involvement by the teaching faculty and less formal means of suggestion and recommendation by students.

Materials related to the curriculum are best developed with close cooperation among faculty, students, professional librarians, and other institutional resource personnel. In case the liberal education, graduate study, or professional degree programs, the specialized expertise of the faculty is used to advise about the scope and nature resources. Appropriate materials which support learning in a variety of disciplines are available and include a wide range of factual and interpretive material.

Some, though by no means all, components of this standard are:

6.B.1 Faculty participate in selection, evaluation, and weeding of library materials and other learning resources.

6.B.2 The institution includes libraries and other learning resources in its long-range academic plan.

Standard 6.C. Availability and Use

Books and other forms of learning materials are readily available and used by the institution's academic community, both on and off-campus.

Several patterns of organization, administration, acquisition, storage, and distribution of learning resources have demonstrated their effectiveness in institutions with diverse personnel, physical facilities, and traditions, and different levels of financial support.

Most important is the extent to which faculty and students make use of all kinds of learning resources. An institution needs generous reading, viewing, and study spaces that are available at time periods which are long enough for and convenient to the users.

While neighboring, available centers may augment its resources, an institution cannot rely exclusively, or even largely, on outside or other resources when it does not influence acquisitions to support its own programs or cannot assure continuity, consistency, and effectiveness of service for its students.

Some, though by no means all, components of this standard are:

6.C.1 Collections are readily available and appropriately used.

6.C.2 Students are required to use the library and/or other appropriate learning resources.

6.C.3 If off-campus programs exist, specific written provision is made for students to have ready access to resource collections or their equivalents.

6.C.4 Open hours provide for convenient access to library collections and resource centers.

Standard 6.D. Professional Staff

A professional staff with pertinent expertise is available to assist users of library and other learning resources.

Effective use of learning resources depends on the efforts of adequately prepared professional librarians, learning specialists, and other resource staff, and on the availability of opportunities for professional improvement. The number and specializations of the staff are affected by many factors, including the number of students and faculty, the extent and variety of services provided, availability of nearby off-campus learning centers, and the physical rate of growth of the total operation. To assist users, competent personnel are available whenever the facilities are open.

Some, though by no means all, components of this standard are:

6.D.1 Professional and other staff are adequate in number, properly qualified in various specialty areas, and available as needed to provide technical support.

6.D.2 Professional staff orient students, new faculty, and other users to the library and other learning resources and emphasize continuing instruction.

Reprinted with permission from Western Association of Schools and Colleges, Handbook of Accreditation (Oakland, California: Western Association of Schools and Colleges, 1982), pp. 45-48.

154958

DATE DUE

DATE DUE			
GAYLORD			PRINTED IN U.S.A.

Mission
Statements for
College Libraries

CLIP Note #5

Compiled by

Larry Hardesty
Director of Library Services
Eckerd College

Jamie Hastreiter
Systems Planning/Serials Coordinator
Eckerd College

David Henderson
Instructional Services/Collection Management Coordinator
Eckerd College

College Library Information Packet Commitee
College Libraries Section
Association of College and Research Libraries
a division of the American Library Association